I0797685

ANIMAL ENCYCLOPEDIAS

THE ARCTIC ANIMAL ENCYCLOPEDIA

BY ASHLEY KUEHL

An Imprint of Abdo Reference
abdobooks.com

TABLE OF CONTENTS

WELCOME TO THE ARCTIC

The Arctic is the northernmost area of Earth. It's a region of extreme cold, ice, and dry weather. Along with Antarctica, the Arctic is one of Earth's two polar regions. Although summer temperatures in the Arctic average around 50°F (10°C), winter temperatures can drop as low as –60°F (–51.1°C).

The Lofoten Islands in Norway are part of the Arctic.

Northern lights dance across the sky in the frozen Arctic.

Most of the Arctic is over the Arctic Ocean. Because the region is so cold, there's a thick sheet of ice on the ocean's surface during most of the year. The North Pole, the most northern point on Earth, is in the middle of the Arctic Circle.

A smaller portion of the Arctic is land, which surrounds the ice sheet and ocean. This land includes parts of several countries, including Greenland, Canada, and Siberia in Russia. Svalbard, a Norwegian archipelago, or group of islands, is in the Arctic too.

During the summer months in the Arctic, there are many hours of daylight and few hours of darkness. On the one-day summer solstice in June, the sun does not set at all. During the winter, on the other hand, daylight hours are few. The winter solstice in December has 24 hours of complete darkness.

Habitats in the Arctic include sea ice, seawater, tundra, forests, and grasslands. Many areas are arid, with only about

Arctic winters have few daylight hours, and the sun stays low on the horizon.

7 inches (17.8 cm) of rain or snow per year. Much of the Arctic is above the tree line, an area where trees stop growing. But smaller plants, including shrubs, lichens, and grass, are able to survive there.

The animals that live in the Arctic have adapted to living in extreme conditions. Some animals spend summers having young in the Arctic. Then they migrate south to warmer areas for winter. Other animals are able to find food and survive in the Arctic year-round.

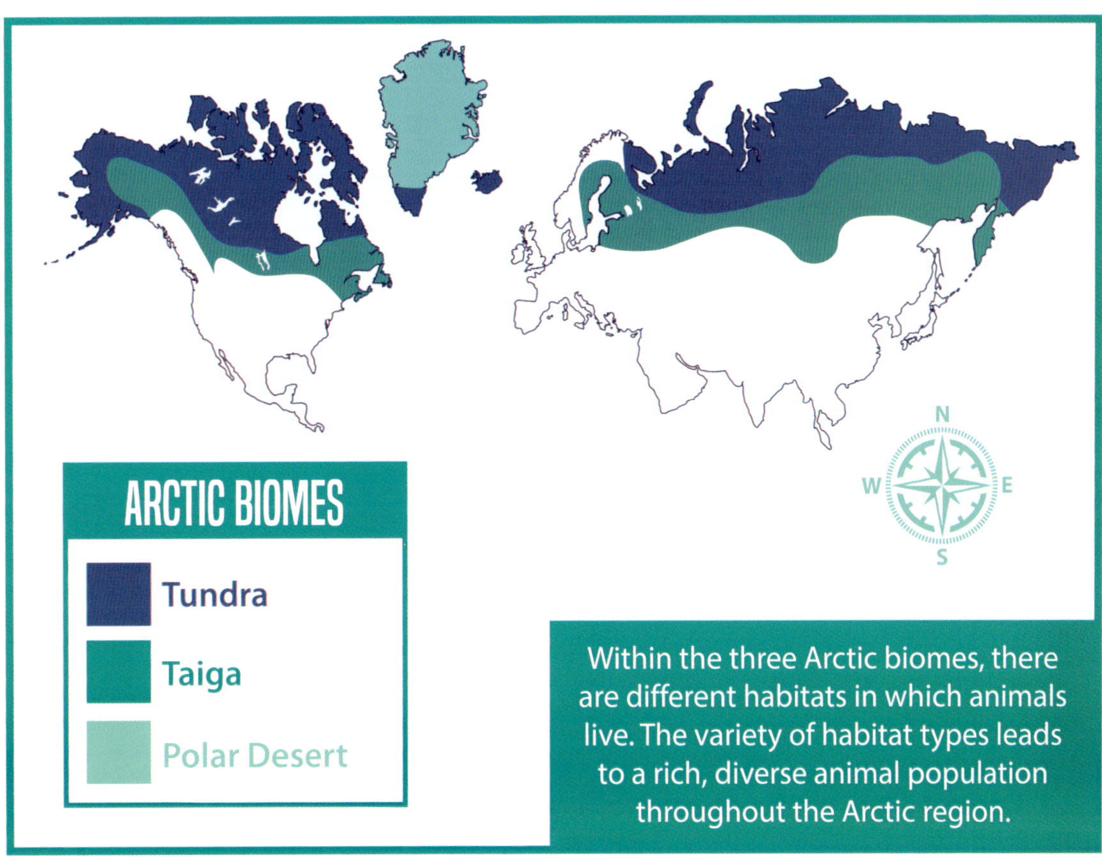

Within the three Arctic biomes, there are different habitats in which animals live. The variety of habitat types leads to a rich, diverse animal population throughout the Arctic region.

MAMMALS

The Arctic fox has thick winter fur and small ears that help it survive the harsh Arctic conditions.

Mammals are vertebrates, which are animals with backbones. Most mammals give birth to live young, rather than laying eggs. Baby mammals drink milk from their mothers' bodies. All mammals have hair or fur covering some or most of their skin.

Mammals are warm-blooded. They can make their own body heat and keep their body at a stable temperature. Mammals live around the world and in a wide range of climates and habitats.

Mammals vary widely in size, shape, appearance, diet, and behavior. Some mammals eat only plants. Carnivorous mammals eat animals. Omnivores eat both plants and animals. Some mammals live in groups. Others are solitary. Mammals move in different ways. Some can swim, whereas others walk, crawl, run, fly, or climb. Mammals in the Arctic include whales, wolves, bears, weasels, dolphins, and walruses.

A humpback whale breaches in Alaska.

BEARDED SEAL

ALL ABOUT

Bearded seals are pinnipeds, a group of animals that includes seals, sea lions, and walruses. These seals are named for their long white whiskers, which are used to look for food on the ocean floor.

- **Length:** 7 to 8 feet (2.1 to 2.4 m)
- **Weight:** 575 to 800 pounds (260.8 to 362.9 kg)
- **Lifespan:** 25 years
- **Conservation Status:** Least Concern

HABITAT & DIET

They live on and around sea ice throughout the Arctic. These seals dive through holes in the ice to find food, which includes clams, shrimp, crabs, and fish such as sculpin and cod.

FAMILY & SOCIAL LIFE

Bearded seals are usually solitary except when mating or raising pups. Females have one pup at a time.

FUN FACT

Bearded seals sometimes sleep upright in the water, resting their head on the ice.

DID YOU KNOW?

Bowhead whales can use their head to break through ice 8 inches (20.3 cm) thick.

BOWHEAD WHALE

ALL ABOUT

The bowhead whale is one of the biggest whales. Its head alone can be more than 16 feet (4.9 m) long.

- **Length:** 50 to 60 feet (15.2 to 18.3 m)
- **Weight:** 75 to 100 tons (68 to 90.7 mt)
- **Lifespan:** more than 200 years
- **Conservation Status:** Least Concern

HABITAT & DIET

Bowhead whales live near northeastern Canada, eastern Greenland, and eastern Siberia. To feed, this whale strains ocean water through its baleen plates, which look like combs. As water filters out, food, such as krill, plankton, and small fish, is trapped in the whale's baleen plates.

FAMILY & SOCIAL LIFE

A bowhead whale calf can swim when it is born. It stays with its mother for about a year.

DALL'S PORPOISE

ALL ABOUT

The largest of all porpoises, Dall's porpoise is playful and curious. It has black-and-white markings, similar to those of an orca.

- **Length:** 7 to 8 feet (2.1 to 2.4 m)
- **Weight:** up to 440 pounds (199.6 kg)
- **Lifespan:** 15 to 20 years
- **Conservation Status:** Least Concern

FUN FACT

The Dall's porpoise can swim up to 34 miles per hour (54.7 kmh).

HABITAT & DIET

These porpoises dive deep to find food, usually at night. They eat herring, hake, anchovies, lanternfish, squid, octopuses, and sometimes crustaceans. They are found in the North Pacific Ocean.

FAMILY & SOCIAL LIFE

Dall's porpoises often swim in groups of 2 to 12. At times, they swim in larger groups and with other dolphins or whales. Dall's porpoises communicate using whistling and clicking sounds.

EURASIAN OTTER

ALL ABOUT

The Eurasian otter has gray-brown fur and webbed feet with claws. It has a long, thin body and a thick tail. It uses its coarse whiskers to find food.

- **Length:** up to 51.2 inches (130 cm)
- **Weight:** up to 19.8 pounds (9 kg)
- **Lifespan:** 5 to 10 years
- **Conservation Status:** Near Threatened

FUN FACT

The Eurasian otter can close its nose and ears when swimming underwater.

HABITAT & DIET

In the Arctic, the Eurasian otter lives in freshwater rivers in northern Asia and Europe. It eats fish, crustaceans, frogs, and birds.

FAMILY & SOCIAL LIFE

Eurasian otters mostly live alone except while mating and raising young. Females make underground burrows to have cubs, two or three at a time. They can breed and have young any time of year.

HARBOR SEAL

ALL ABOUT

Harbor seals, like other seals, have short flippers. They have small snouts. When they're not hunting, they often rest out of the water. Staying in groups helps keep them safe from predators.

- **Length:** 4.5 to 6 feet (1.4 to 1.8 m)
- **Weight:** 180 to 285 pounds (81.6 to 129.3 kg)
- **Lifespan:** 25 to 30 years
- **Conservation Status:** Least Concern

DID YOU KNOW?

Harbor seals move their bodies in waves, like caterpillars. That's because the bones in their pelvis are attached and can't move.

HABITAT & DIET

Harbor seals dive to hunt for food. They eat crustaceans, shellfish, and fish. They live in northern oceans, near coastlines of Asia, Europe, and North America. But they can also live in fresh water.

FAMILY & SOCIAL LIFE

Pups can swim as soon as they are born. Mothers sometimes gather in groups to care for pups collectively.

HARP SEAL

FUN FACT

Harp seal mothers identify their pups in large groups by their smell.

ALL ABOUT

Harp seal pups are born with white fur, but adults have gray fur with black patches on their sides. Adult harp seals shed their fur in the springtime.

- **Length:** 5 to 6 feet (1.5 to 1.8 m)
- **Weight:** 260 to 300 pounds (117.9 to 136.1 kg)
- **Lifespan:** 30 years
- **Conservation Status:** Least Concern

HABITAT & DIET

Harp seals spend most of their time in cold water in the Arctic and North Atlantic Oceans. They can stay underwater for about 15 minutes at a time. They eat fish and invertebrates. They can dive 1,300 feet (396.2 m) deep.

FAMILY & SOCIAL LIFE

During breeding season, harp seals migrate north. Big groups, sometimes made of thousands of individuals, gather on the ice to mate.

HOODED SEAL

ALL ABOUT

Hooded seals are gray with dark splotches on their bodies. But their most distinctive feature is a red sac in the male's nose. When inflated, it can cover the seal's face and head, like a hood. This hood helps attract the attention of female seals. Males also use their hood to compete with other males.

- **Length:** 6.5 to 8.5 feet (2 to 2.6 m)
- **Weight:** 320 to 776 pounds (145.2 to 352 kg)
- **Lifespan:** 25 to 35 years
- **Conservation Status:** Vulnerable

DID YOU KNOW?

Many people hunt hooded seal pups for their fur. This has put the seals' population at risk.

HABITAT & DIET

Hooded seals eat cod, halibut, herring, sea stars, mussels, and squid. They can dive up to 3,280 feet (999.7 m) below the water's surface to find food. They stay underwater for up to an hour at a time. Hooded seals can be found in the North Atlantic and Arctic Oceans.

FAMILY & SOCIAL LIFE

Unlike most seals, hooded seals tend to live alone, except during mating season when large groups gather on ice to breed. Pups drink their mothers' milk for about four days. During that time, their body weight doubles. After that, pups are left to feed themselves.

NARWHAL

ALL ABOUT

A narwhal is a toothed whale, but it has no visible teeth in its mouth. Instead, the male has one long, spiral tooth that sticks out of its jaw. This tooth, or tusk, can be 9.8 feet (3 m) long. It is a large canine tooth that grows through the narwhal's upper lip.

- **Length:** 13 to 20 feet (4 to 6.1 m)
- **Weight:** 1.5 tons (1.4 mt)
- **Lifespan:** up to 50 years
- **Conservation Status:** Least Concern

DID YOU KNOW?

Hundreds of years ago, whale hunters returning home with narwhal tusks told stories about the animals, including many unicorn legends.

FUN FACT

On rare occasions, a female narwhal will grow a tusk, or a male may grow two.

HABITAT & DIET

Narwhals can dive deeper than most mammals. They spend much of their time deeper than 2,625 feet (800.1 m). But they are able to dive down to 5,905 feet (1,799.8 m). Narwhals eat cod, shrimp, squid, and halibut. They eat more in the winter and less in the summer. They live throughout the Arctic Ocean.

FAMILY & SOCIAL LIFE

Narwhals travel in groups of at least 15, but they sometimes gather by the hundreds or thousands. Young usually stay with their mother for at least a year.

ORCA

ALL ABOUT

Orcas are sometimes called killer whales, but they are, in fact, the largest dolphin species. Orcas can swim as fast as 33.5 miles per hour (53.9 kmh). They live in oceans all around the world. These huge creatures are mostly black with distinctive white patches.

- **Length:** up to 32 feet (9.8 m)
- **Weight:** 11 tons (10 mt)
- **Lifespan:** up to 90 years
- **Conservation Status:** Data Deficient

FUN FACT

Orcas are thought to be one of the most intelligent animal species on Earth.

DID YOU KNOW?

From one generation to the next, orcas will pass certain behaviors, including hunting strategies for particular prey.

HABITAT & DIET

Orcas eat many kinds of sea animals, including salmon, seals, squid, birds, and whales. They work together to hunt in groups. They use echolocation to communicate with one another and to find prey.

FAMILY & SOCIAL LIFE

Orcas live together in pods of usually 3 to 20 members. Orcas stay together for many years. Females have one calf at a time. The young can swim right away, but they stay with their mother for up to two years. Sometimes a young orca stays with its mother's pod. Other times it joins another pod once it's grown.

POLAR BEAR

ALL ABOUT

The largest species of bears, polar bears spend their lives on sea ice and in cold ocean waters across the Arctic. They are excellent swimmers, using their front legs to paddle and their back legs to steer. A thick layer of blubber and dense fur keep them warm. Large paws and sharp claws help them walk on ice as well as catch prey.

- **Length:** 6 to 9 feet (1.8 to 2.7 m)
- **Weight:** 300 to 1,300 pounds (136.1 to 589.7 kg)
- **Lifespan:** 25 to 30 years
- **Conservation Status:** Vulnerable

HABITAT & DIET

Polar bears can smell their prey, mostly ringed and bearded seals, from up to 9.9 miles (15.9 km) away. These bears also eat fish, birds, eggs, baby animals, and carrion. To hunt a seal, a polar bear waits next to a hole in the ice. When a seal comes up for air, the polar bear attacks.

FAMILY & SOCIAL LIFE

In winter, females give birth to one to four cubs in snow dens. The family emerges from the den four or five months later. Cubs stay with their mother for about two years, while they learn survival and hunting skills.

DID YOU KNOW?

Because they spend much of their time on sea ice, polar bears are classified as marine mammals.

FUN FACT

The polar bear has white fur, but its skin is black. It also has a blue tongue.

RIBBON SEAL

ALL ABOUT

Adult ribbon seals have black bodies with four yellow or white bands. The bands develop over the first few years of their life.

- **Length:** 5 to 6 feet (1.5 to 1.8 m)
- **Weight:** 200 to 330 pounds (90.7 to 149.7 kg)
- **Lifespan:** 20 to 30 years
- **Conservation Status:** Least Concern

DID YOU KNOW?

Ribbon seals have an internal air sac connected to their windpipe. It may help the seals dive and float or make sounds.

HABITAT & DIET

These seals spend late winter through early summer on sea ice in the southern Arctic and North Pacific Oceans, where they rest and have pups. Ribbon seals eat fish, cephalopods, and crustaceans. Young pups eat mostly tiny invertebrates.

FAMILY & SOCIAL LIFE

Except during breeding season, ribbon seals mostly live alone. Females have one pup at a time. The pups nurse for three to four weeks before they are left to care for themselves.

SEA OTTER

ALL ABOUT

Sea otters have the densest fur of any animal on Earth. They spend much of their time floating on the ocean surface while sleeping, eating, grooming, or caring for young.

- **Length:** up to 5 feet (1.5 m)
- **Weight:** 50 to 100 pounds (22.7 to 45.4 kg)
- **Lifespan:** up to 23 years
- **Conservation Status:** Endangered

DID YOU KNOW?

Sea otters sometimes hold paws to stay together while floating. They also wrap themselves in kelp so they don't float away.

HABITAT & DIET

Sea otters live in coastal areas around Alaska and the Bering Sea. They eat crabs, sea urchins, clams, and mussels. Sea otters open shelled animals by striking them with rocks.

FAMILY & SOCIAL LIFE

Sea otters gather in groups called rafts. A pup's dense fur keeps the pup afloat. It can only dive once its adult fur has grown in.

SPOTTED SEAL

ALL ABOUT

The spotted seal has brown-and-black spots all over its body. It lives in the North Pacific Ocean, between Asia and North America. The seal migrates between sea ice in the north and coastlines farther south.

- **Length:** 4.5 to 5.5 feet (1.4 to 1.7 m)
- **Weight:** 140 to 250 pounds (63.5 to 113.4 kg)
- **Lifespan:** 30 to 35 years
- **Conservation Status:** Least Concern to Near Threatened

HABITAT & DIET

Spotted seals breed on floating pieces of ice. Young spotted seals mostly eat crustaceans. Adults primarily eat fish, including herring and walleye pollock.

FAMILY & SOCIAL LIFE

Females have one pup at a time. They mate four to six weeks after the pups are born. The next pup is born about 10 months later.

FUN FACT

During breeding season, spotted seals form family groups of one female, one male, and their pup.

STELLER SEA LION

ALL ABOUT

Steller sea lions, also called northern sea lions, can turn their hind flippers forward to move on land. Their long front flippers propel the sea lions through the water when swimming.

- **Length:** 7.5 to 11 feet (2.3 to 3.4 m)
- **Weight:** 800 to 2,500 pounds (362.9 to 1,134 kg)
- **Lifespan:** 18 to 30 years
- **Conservation Status:** Near Threatened

HABITAT & DIET

Steller sea lions can be found in the northern Pacific Ocean. They eat a variety of fish, squid, and octopuses.

FUN FACT

Steller sea lions are good at climbing and can climb cliff faces.

FAMILY & SOCIAL LIFE

Steller sea lions rest and breed in large groups on land, sometimes lying on top of one another. A group on land is called a colony. A group at sea is called a raft.

WALRUS

ALL ABOUT

Walruses have tusks that can grow 3 feet (0.9 m) long. These tusks, which are long teeth, are used for defense, for making breathing holes, and for hauling the animals onto the ice.

- **Length:** 7.25 to 11.5 feet (2.2 to 3.5 m)
- **Weight:** 881.8 to 3,968.3 pounds (400 to 1,800 kg)
- **Lifespan:** up to 40 years
- **Conservation Status:** Vulnerable

HABITAT & DIET

Walruses live mostly on ice near the Arctic Circle. Walruses can walk on land or ice and swim in water. Their whiskers help them find food on the ocean floor. They eat mollusks, invertebrates, worms, and fish. For shelled prey, the walrus squashes the shell with its flippers before swallowing the animal.

DID YOU KNOW?

Walruses have an inflatable air sac on their throat. This allows a walrus to sleep in the water while keeping its head afloat, preventing drowning.

FAMILY & SOCIAL LIFE

Walruses spend time in large groups of hundreds to more than a thousand. They bellow and snort to communicate. They mate in water but have babies on land. Pups stay with their mother for two to three years.

FUN FACT

Walruses can slow down their heartbeats. That helps them survive in cold water.

WHITE WHALE

ALL ABOUT

The white whale, or beluga whale, is one of the smallest whales. It has a thick layer of fat called blubber that helps it stay warm in cold Arctic waters. These whales use their strong sense of hearing and echolocation to hunt.

- **Length:** 8.5 to 22 feet (2.6 to 6.7 m)
- **Weight:** 1,500 to 3,500 pounds (680.4 to 1,587.6 kg)
- **Lifespan:** 35 to 50 years
- **Conservation Status:** Least Concern

HABITAT & DIET

White whales eat fish including cod, herring, and salmon. They also eat octopuses, clams, snails, shrimp, and crabs. Scientists use the layers of a white whale's teeth to estimate its age. They live in the Arctic Ocean and nearby seas.

DID YOU KNOW?

The white whale can move its melon, or forehead area, allowing it to change its facial expressions.

FAMILY & SOCIAL LIFE

White whales are social animals and communicate by making sounds such as whistles, clicks, and chirps. They are often called the canaries of the sea.

These mammals travel together in pods. Some pods have hundreds of whales. They spend summer in the Arctic waters. When sea ice builds up in winter, the whales migrate south. After a pregnancy that lasts about 15 months, a female gives birth to usually one calf every three years.

FUN FACT

At birth, the white whale is dark gray. Its color grows lighter as it ages.

ARCTIC FOX

ALL ABOUT

Arctic foxes have mostly white fur in the winter. In summer, their fur turns brown or gray. These colors help them camouflage with the seasons. The fox's thick tail helps it balance and stay warm.

- **Length:** 18 to 26.8 inches (45.7 to 68.1 cm)
- **Weight:** 6.5 to 17 pounds (2.9 to 7.7 kg)
- **Lifespan:** 3 to 6 years
- **Conservation Status:** Least Concern

An Arctic fox's thick, furry paws help it walk on snow and ice.

Arctic foxes can smell a seal den from a mile away.

HABITAT & DIET

Arctic foxes live in many areas of the Arctic tundra, where they hunt birds, fish, and rodents. These foxes sometimes trail polar bears to eat their leftovers. Arctic foxes live in burrows and will dig into deep snow to make shelters.

FAMILY & SOCIAL LIFE

In the spring, a female may have as many as 20 pups. They leave the den in autumn to live on their own. Arctic foxes mate for life.

ARCTIC WOLF

ALL ABOUT

Arctic wolves have thick white coats, furry paws, and small noses and ears. These adaptations help them stay warm in cold Arctic winters.

- **Length:** 3 to 5.9 feet (0.9 to 1.8 m)
- **Weight:** 70.4 to 154 pounds (31.9 to 69.9 kg)
- **Lifespan:** 7 to 17 years
- **Conservation Status:** Least Concern

FUN FACT

Arctic wolves can smell an animal three days after it has left an area.

HABITAT & DIET

Arctic wolves live in remote tundras in Canada, Alaska, and Greenland. They hunt musk oxen, Arctic hares, caribou, birds, and lemmings.

FAMILY & SOCIAL LIFE

Arctic wolves travel and hunt in packs of 7 to 10. Each pack has two alphas, a male and a female. The female alpha has two or three pups at a time. The whole pack cares for the pups.

RED FOX

ALL ABOUT

Red foxes have a red back, face, and tail. Their chin and belly are whitish gray. The tip of their tail is white.

- **Length:** 18 to 33.75 inches (45.7 to 85.7 cm)
- **Weight:** 6.5 to 24 pounds (2.9 to 10.9 kg)
- **Lifespan:** 2 to 4 years
- **Conservation Status:** Least Concern

FUN FACT

A red fox can hear animals digging underground.

HABITAT & DIET

Red foxes live in woodlands, wetlands, and fields around the world, usually in open areas. They hunt rabbits, rodents, and birds. They will also eat fruit.

FAMILY & SOCIAL LIFE

These foxes usually live and hunt alone. They mate in winter. Then the female builds a den and has between 2 and 12 pups. The pups stay with both parents until fall before becoming independent.

CANADA LYNX

ALL ABOUT

The Canada lynx has big, round feet with fur on the bottom. Its feet, along with its long hind legs, help the lynx travel through deep snow.

- **Length:** 30 to 35 inches (76.2 to 88.9 cm)
- **Weight:** 15 to 30 pounds (6.8 to 13.6 kg)
- **Lifespan:** up to 14 years
- **Conservation Status:** Least Concern

HABITAT & DIET

These cats live in snow-covered forests in Alaska and Canada. The lynx mostly hunts snowshoe hares, usually killing one every couple of days. This lynx will also hunt grouse and rodents.

FAMILY & SOCIAL LIFE

Canada lynx mostly live alone. After mating, mothers care for the kittens and teach them to hunt. A female usually has one to five kittens at a time.

DID YOU KNOW?

The Canada lynx's winter coat is thick and gray. Its summer coat is thin and reddish brown.

EURASIAN LYNX

ALL ABOUT

The biggest species of lynx, the Eurasian lynx makes a variety of sounds, including growling, grunting, hissing, purring, and meowing.

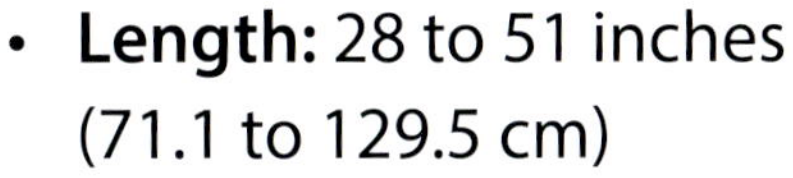

- **Length:** 28 to 51 inches (71.1 to 129.5 cm)
- **Weight:** 40 to 80 pounds (18.1 to 36.3 kg)
- **Lifespan:** up to 17 years
- **Conservation Status:** Least Concern

DID YOU KNOW?

The Eurasian lynx grows extra thick fur on its paws in winter, helping it travel through deep snow.

HABITAT & DIET

The Eurasian lynx lives in forests, mountains, and tundra areas in Russia, northern Europe, central Asia, and the Arctic. It eats rodents, hares, birds and eggs, musk deer, and roe deer. The lynx usually lies in wait for its prey and then attacks.

FAMILY & SOCIAL LIFE

Males travel and hunt alone. After mating, females find a den to have up to four kittens. Young Eurasian lynx stay in the den with their mother until they are 10 months old.

CARIBOU

ALL ABOUT

Caribou are large animals with big antlers that males use for fighting. Caribou also have broad, furry hooves with sharp edges. Their hooves are used to dig for plants, to grip icy ground, and to swim. In winter, caribou have thick, warm fur. In spring, this fur falls out and lighter summer fur comes in.

- **Height:** 4 to 5 feet (1.2 to 1.5 m)
- **Weight:** 175 to 400 pounds (79.4 to 181.4 kg)
- **Lifespan:** 15 to 18 years
- **Conservation Status:** Vulnerable

FUN FACT

Caribou can run up to 50 miles per hour (80.5 kmh).

HABITAT & DIET

Caribou spend winter in forests in Canada, Alaska, and northern Asia and Europe, but they are constantly on the move searching for food. They eat plants, including grass, herbs, moss, shrubs, and trees. In the winter, they sometimes scrape snow off the ground to find lichens and mushrooms.

FAMILY & SOCIAL LIFE

In spring, large caribou herds migrate north to the tundra. Females have one calf each year. Some are born at the end of the migration. Others are born while the herd is on the move. Calves can walk at one day old, which enables them to migrate with their mother.

DID YOU KNOW?

A male caribou's antlers can grow up to 51 inches (129.5 cm) long. A female's can grow up to 20 inches (50.8 cm). The antlers of both males and females fall off and grow back every year.

DALL'S SHEEP

ALL ABOUT

Dall's sheep are large hoofed animals with white coats. Adult males have distinctive curled horns, which they use to fight to clarify their rank, or status, in the group. Sometimes the males also kick or charge one another.

- **Length:** 4.3 to 5.9 feet (1.3 to 1.8 m)
- **Weight:** up to 300 pounds (136.1 kg)
- **Lifespan:** 11 to 14 years
- **Conservation Status:** Least Concern

FUN FACT

The age of a Dall's sheep can be determined by counting the rings on its horns.

HABITAT & DIET

Dall's sheep live on mountains in dry areas of Alaska and Canada. To stay safe from predators, they move to very steep hills, rocks, or ridges. They eat many kinds of plants, including moss, lichens, sedges, and grass.

FAMILY & SOCIAL LIFE

Males and females generally live separately, other than during mating season. To prepare for birth, females find safe, private places on rugged cliffs. They have one lamb per year. Mothers and lambs stay together on their cliffs for a few days. Lambs begin eating plants within their first week. Mothers and lambs often group together to help care for the young.

DID YOU KNOW?

Male Dall's sheep have an extra layer of bone on their head that protects them during fights.

MOOSE

ALL ABOUT

Moose are the biggest members of the deer family. They are dark brown or black with long legs. A flap of skin, called a bell or a dewlap, hangs from their neck. Sometimes bears and wolves attack moose with young calves. The moose may run or swim away. Or they may attack the predator with their legs.

- **Height:** 5 to 7 feet (1.5 to 2.1 m)
- **Weight:** 660 to 1,300 pounds (299.4 to 589.7 kg)
- **Lifespan:** 15 to 20 years
- **Conservation Status:** Least Concern

FUN FACT

A moose's antlers can be 6 feet (1.8 m) wide.

DID YOU KNOW?

The biggest moose live in Siberia and Alaska. They can be 7 feet (2.1 m) tall.

HABITAT & DIET

Moose usually live in forests in Asia, Europe, and North America, near ponds and streams. They eat both land plants and water plants. In winter, they eat pine cones and shrubs, as well as lichens and moss.

FAMILY & SOCIAL LIFE

Females have one or two calves at a time. The calves stay with their mother for a year.

Males frequently fight during mating season, in September and October. Males lose their antlers in winter and grow new ones in the spring. Females don't have antlers.

MUSK OX

ALL ABOUT

Musk oxen have big heads and short legs. They have two layers of long, shaggy fur. In the summer, the layer underneath falls out. It grows back in time for winter. Although this animal is named the musk ox, it is more closely related to sheep and goats. Both male and female musk oxen have horns.

- **Height:** 4 to 5 feet (1.2 to 1.5 m)
- **Weight:** 500 to 800 pounds (226.8 to 362.9 kg)
- **Lifespan:** 12 to 20 years
- **Conservation Status:** Least Concern

DID YOU KNOW?

People in the Arctic use musk oxen fur to make soft yarn.

HABITAT & DIET

Musk oxen live in the Arctic tundra. In winter, they eat lichens, moss, and roots. In summer, they also eat grass and flowers.

FAMILY & SOCIAL LIFE

Mating season happens in late summer. Males battle by charging and crashing into one another. The winner gets to mate with the herd. The next spring, females each have one calf.

Musk oxen group together in herds of two to three dozen. If a predator tries to attack, the herd makes a circle. The musk oxen face out, keeping their calves in the middle.

FUN FACT

This animal's name comes from its musky smell.

SNOW SHEEP

ALL ABOUT

Snow sheep have wide heads and short legs. They expertly maneuver across rocky, steep cliffs. Their thick and shaggy gray coats provide warmth in the winter. In the summer, their coats become darker brown and smooth. Males are bigger than females.

- **Length:** 49.6 to 74 inches (126 to 188 cm)
- **Weight:** 132 to 330 pounds (59.9 to 149.7 kg)
- **Lifespan:** 9 years
- **Conservation Status:** Least Concern

HABITAT & DIET

The snow sheep can be found in the meadows and mountains of eastern Siberia, the only place it lives. Winter temperatures can get as cold as –67°F (–55°C). Snow sheep eat grass, shrubs, lichens, moss, and mushrooms. But if there's too much snow, it's difficult to find food.

FAMILY & SOCIAL LIFE

Female snow sheep give birth to one lamb at a time. Snow sheep form small groups. One type of group is mothers and their young. Young males group together, and older males group together too.

DID YOU KNOW?

Many snow sheep lambs are killed by predators or die from Siberia's harsh weather within their first year of life.

FUN FACT

The size of a male's horns usually determines his rank in the group.

ALASKA MARMOT

ALL ABOUT

A marmot is a large type of ground squirrel. Marmots have strong claws, short legs, and thick fur.

- **Length:** 21.2 to 25.7 inches (53.8 to 65.3 cm)
- **Weight:** 5.5 to 8.8 pounds (2.5 to 4 kg)
- **Lifespan:** 13 to 15 years
- **Conservation Status:** Least Concern

The Alaska marmot rubs its face on rocks to mark its territory.

HABITAT & DIET

Alaska marmots live in mountain valleys and canyons in northern Alaska. They eat grass, flowers, lichens, and berries.

FAMILY & SOCIAL LIFE

During the winter, the Alaska marmot hibernates in dens they dig between rocks. Tunnels between dens connect colonies. Females give birth to between three and eight young. They stay with their parents for two years.

ARCTIC GROUND SQUIRREL

ALL ABOUT

The Arctic ground squirrel has short front legs and claws, used for digging. Their back legs are short and strong, helping them move.

- **Length:** 13 to 19.5 inches (33 to 49.5 cm)
- **Weight:** 1.2 to 3.3 pounds (0.5 to 1.5 kg)
- **Lifespan:** 8 to 10 years
- **Conservation Status:** Least Concern

FUN FACT

Before hibernation, about one-third of Arctic ground squirrels' bodies are stored fat.

HABITAT & DIET

They live in tundras, forests, and meadows in Alaska and northern Canada. During their seven to eight months of hibernation, their body temperature can drop to 26.8°F (–2.9°C).

FAMILY & SOCIAL LIFE

Arctic ground squirrels live in colonies. They work together to dig underground burrow systems, where they hide from predators, hibernate, and care for young.

BLACK-CAPPED MARMOT

ALL ABOUT

Black-capped marmots have black fur on their heads. They shed and regrow their fur every year.

- **Length:** 17.7 to 20.1 inches (45 to 51.1 cm)
- **Weight:** 4.4 to 16.5 pounds (2 to 7.5 kg)
- **Lifespan:** about 15 years
- **Conservation Status:** Least Concern

HABITAT & DIET

Black-capped marmots live at high altitudes in northern Russia. They eat plants including grass, berries, and seeds. They often live on grassy or rocky south-facing mountainsides, which get a lot of sunlight. In the winter, they hibernate in burrows.

FUN FACT

Black-capped marmots build complex tunnel systems, which can be 370.7 feet (113 m) long.

FAMILY & SOCIAL LIFE

Black-capped marmots live in small family groups. A group consists of one male and one female that mate and produce young, along with a few younger marmots that don't breed.

CANADIAN LEMMING

ALL ABOUT

Lemmings are brown and gray, with short legs and tails. The Canadian lemming is also known as the Nearctic brown lemming. Populations of lemmings can fluctuate from year to year.

- **Length:** 4.7 inches (11.9 cm)
- **Weight:** 2.1 ounces (59.5 g)
- **Lifespan:** 1 year
- **Conservation Status:** Least Concern

HABITAT & DIET

Canadian lemmings live in the tundra, meadows, and bogs in northern Canada. They eat grass, sedges, moss, and willows. In winter, lemmings use grass and sedges to build large nests underneath the snow to insulate themselves from the cold.

FAMILY & SOCIAL LIFE

Lemmings can have up to three litters in a year. Each litter has four to nine babies.

DID YOU KNOW?

Many animals prey on lemmings. When lemming populations are low, predator populations drop as well.

NORTHERN COLLARED LEMMING

ALL ABOUT

The northern collared lemming has gray summer fur with black stripes on its head and back. In winter, these lemmings shed their summer fur for a warmer white coat.

- **Length:** 5.1 to 6.3 inches (13 to 16 cm)
- **Weight:** 1.6 to 4 ounces (45.4 to 113.4 g)
- **Lifespan:** about 2 years
- **Conservation Status:** Least Concern

HABITAT & DIET

These lemmings live in open, dry tundra in Alaska, Greenland, and northern Canada. They eat plants, including lichens, seeds, berries, roots, and willow tree bark.

FAMILY & SOCIAL LIFE

Collared lemmings tend to live alone. In the winter, they spend time in their underground burrows. Females can have two or three litters in a year.

FUN FACT

The northern collared lemming's front teeth keep growing for the animal's whole life.

TUNDRA VOLE

ALL ABOUT

Voles at higher elevations tend to be bigger and have smaller tails. Their strongest senses are hearing and smell.

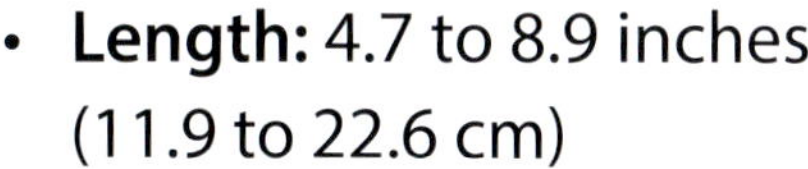

- **Length:** 4.7 to 8.9 inches (11.9 to 22.6 cm)
- **Weight:** 0.9 to 2.8 ounces (25.5 to 79.4 g)
- **Lifespan:** 1 to 2 years
- **Conservation Status:** Least Concern

FUN FACT

Females can mate and have young starting at three weeks old.

HABITAT & DIET

Tundra voles live near lakes and streams in forests, tundras, and meadows in Asia, northwestern North America, and parts of Europe. They eat mostly sedges, but they also eat herbs, shrubs, lichens, and moss. In fall, they collect and store seeds for winter.

FAMILY & SOCIAL LIFE

Females can have two or three litters of four to eight young in a year, usually between April and September.

ADDITIONAL MAMMALS

ALASKAN HARE

ALL ABOUT

Alaskan hares live on the western side of Alaska. Males and females are the same size. Their ears are short, which helps them keep warm.

- **Length:** 19.7 to 27.6 inches (50 to 70.1 cm)
- **Weight:** 8.6 to 15.9 pounds (3.9 to 7.2 kg)
- **Lifespan:** 4 to 5 years
- **Conservation Status:** Least Concern

FUN FACT

The Alaskan hare's fur changes from reddish brown in summer to white in winter.

HABITAT & DIET

The Alaskan hare lives mostly in tundras or on rocky slopes, in areas with many plants. They eat shrubs and berries.

FAMILY & SOCIAL LIFE

During mating season, these hares form big groups. Other times, they mostly live alone. Females have young in nests above the ground. They have one litter of four to eight babies in the summer.

AMERICAN MINK

ALL ABOUT

Minks are good at climbing and swimming. They are more active at night than during the day. They have long, thin bodies with short legs and partially webbed feet.

- **Length:** 18.1 to 27.6 inches (46 to 70.1 cm)
- **Weight:** 1.5 to 3.5 pounds (0.7 to 1.6 kg)
- **Lifespan:** 10 years
- **Conservation Status:** Least Concern

FUN FACT

When a mink is excited or scared, it releases a stinky liquid.

HABITAT & DIET

American minks usually live in forests near lakes, ponds, or streams across North America. They dig burrows in riverbanks or occupy abandoned dens from other animals. They eat frogs, crayfish, shrews, mice, rabbits, and fish.

FAMILY & SOCIAL LIFE

Minks mate in the winter and have young in the spring. Females raise up to eight babies in a litter.

ARCTIC HARE

ALL ABOUT

The Arctic hare has bluish-gray fur in summer that changes to bright white in the winter. The white winter hairs are hollow, which helps with insulation. Fur on the bottoms of the hares' feet provide warmth and support while walking across snow.

- **Length:** 19 to 26 inches (48.3 to 66 cm)
- **Weight:** 6 to 15 pounds (2.7 to 6.8 kg)
- **Lifespan:** up to 5 years
- **Conservation Status:** Least Concern

FUN FACT

An Arctic hare can move as fast as 40 miles per hour (64.6 kmh).

HABITAT & DIET

Arctic hares live in the tundras of northern Canada and Greenland. They eat lichens, woody plants, moss, berries, leaves, and bark.

FAMILY & SOCIAL LIFE

Arctic hares sometimes travel alone, but they also form groups or pairs during mating season. Females have up to two litters of two to eight young each year.

BROWN BEAR

ALL ABOUT

Brown bears are large animals with thick brown fur. They have long, straight claws, which help them dig for roots or small animals.

- **Length:** up to 9 feet (2.7 m)
- **Weight:** up to 1,600 pounds (725.7 kg)
- **Lifespan:** 25 years
- **Conservation Status:** Least Concern

HABITAT & DIET

Brown bears eat nuts, leaves, fruit, and roots, as well as fish and mammals. They often live along coastlines in northwestern North America and parts of Asia and Europe.

FUN FACT

In the fall, a brown bear can eat 90 pounds (40.8 kg) of food in a day.

FAMILY & SOCIAL LIFE

Brown bears hibernate in dens in the winter. Females usually have cubs during their hibernation but only once every three years. Cubs stay with their mother for two-and-a-half years. Other than these family groupings, brown bears mostly live alone.

EURASIAN LEAST SHREW

ALL ABOUT

The brown-and-gray Eurasian least shrew is the second smallest mammal on Earth. It is a little larger than the similar Etruscan pygmy shrew, which lives in Mediterranean areas and parts of Asia. They are good swimmers and climbers and have a strong sense of hearing.

- **Length:** up to 2 inches (5.1 cm)
- **Weight:** 0.05 to 0.1 ounces (1.4 to 2.8 g)
- **Lifespan:** less than 2 years
- **Conservation Status:** Least Concern

HABITAT & DIET

This shrew lives in tundra, shrublands, and forests. It eats insects and spiders.

FAMILY & SOCIAL LIFE

Females can have up to three litters per year. Each litter usually has four or five young.

FUN FACT

The Eurasian least shrew sleeps for 10 to 50 minutes at a time.

EURASIAN PYGMY SHREW

FUN FACT

The Eurasian pygmy shrew has red teeth.

ALL ABOUT

The tiny Eurasian pygmy shrew has thin gray or brown fur. It pokes its snout into dirt to find prey.

- **Length:** 1.5 to 2.4 inches (3.8 to 6.1 cm)
- **Weight:** 0.1 to 0.2 ounces (2.8 to 5.7 g)
- **Lifespan:** 1.5 to 2 years
- **Conservation Status:** Least Concern

HABITAT & DIET

This shrew lives in northern Eurasia in areas with many plants, where it hides from predators. It eats more than its own body weight in insects and arthropods every day.

FAMILY & SOCIAL LIFE

Females have their young in nests, often made of grass. They usually have two litters a year, but they can have up to five. Each litter has 4 to 12 babies.

GRIZZLY BEAR

FUN FACT

A grizzly bear can run up to 35 miles per hour (56.3 kmh).

ALL ABOUT

Grizzly bears are a subspecies of brown bears. They live in Alaska and Canada. They have dark or light brown fur with silver tips. They have a large hump on their back.

- **Length:** 5 to 8 feet (1.5 to 2.4 m)
- **Weight:** 800 to 900 pounds (362.9 to 408.2 kg)
- **Lifespan:** 25 years
- **Conservation Status:** Least Concern

HABITAT & DIET

As omnivores, grizzlies eat small mammals, fish, berries, carrion, and plant roots. They mark their territory by rubbing on trees or scratching or biting off bark.

FAMILY & SOCIAL LIFE

Grizzly bears mostly live alone, but cubs stay with their mother for more than two years. These bears communicate with a variety of sounds including growls and grunts.

LEAST WEASEL

ALL ABOUT

The least weasel is a long, tube-shaped animal. It has brown fur in the summer and white fur in the winter.

- **Length:** 6.5 to 8.5 inches (16.5 to 21.6 cm)
- **Weight:** 1.1 to 3.5 ounces (31.2 to 99.2 g)
- **Lifespan:** up to 4 years
- **Conservation Status:** Least Concern

FUN FACT

Least weasels often kill large prey, storing leftover food for later.

HABITAT & DIET

Least weasels can live in many habitats, including forests, tundra, and grasslands throughout the northern hemisphere. They spend time both above and below ground in tunnels. They use other animals' dens to hide when they are hunting.

FAMILY & SOCIAL LIFE

Least weasels usually live and hunt alone, other than during mating season.

MASKED SHREW

ALL ABOUT

Masked shrews are most active at night when hunting. During the day, they hide from predators, often among plants.

- **Length:** 3.9 inches (9.9 cm)
- **Weight:** 0.09 to 0.14 ounces (2.6 to 4 g)
- **Lifespan:** 1 to 2 years
- **Conservation Status:** Least Concern

HABITAT & DIET

The masked shrew lives in a variety of Arctic habitats across Alaska and Canada, including meadows, forests, riverbanks, and lake shores. They eat ants, beetles, spiders, grasshoppers, slugs, insect larvae, seeds, and mushrooms.

FUN FACT

Masked shrews are born without any hair and with their eyelids stuck closed.

FAMILY & SOCIAL LIFE

Masked shrews sometimes fight by standing on their back legs and pushing each other with their front feet. They squeak during these fights.

MOUNTAIN HARE

ALL ABOUT

Mountain hares are brown in the summer and white in the winter. To protect themselves, they sometimes jump sideways, making it challenging for a predator to follow their tracks.

- **Length:** 16.9 to 24 inches (42.9 to 61 cm)
- **Weight:** 2.2 to 8.8 pounds (1 to 4 kg)
- **Lifespan:** 9 years
- **Conservation Status:** Least Concern

DID YOU KNOW?

The mountain hare has three types of fur: underfur, pile hair (in the middle), and guard hair.

HABITAT & DIET

The mountain hare can live in forest, tundra, and moorlands of northern Europe and Asia. They eat leaves, twigs, bark, lichens, grass, and heather.

FAMILY & SOCIAL LIFE

Most females have one or two litters of one to four young in a season. Females that are bigger in size tend to have more babies in a litter.

SABLE

ALL ABOUT

Part of the weasel family, the sable has light or dark brown fur, sometimes with black markings.

- **Length:** 13.8 to 22 inches (35.1 to 55.9 cm)
- **Weight:** 1.5 to 4 pounds (0.7 to 1.8 kg)
- **Lifespan:** 8 to 18 years
- **Conservation Status:** Least Concern

HABITAT & DIET

This creature lives in forests in northern Asia. It eats berries and nuts, but it also hunts rodents, hares, and birds. Sables sometimes eat fish, mollusks, or leftovers from wolf kills.

FAMILY & SOCIAL LIFE

Females make nests from leaves, grass, and moss in hollow trees. They have between one and seven kits at a time. Before the kits are born, males guard the area and bring the mothers food.

SHORT-TAILED WEASEL

ALL ABOUT

Sometimes called a stoat or ermine, the short-tailed weasel is brownish red with a white belly in summer. In the winter, its fur becomes all white with a black tail tip.

- **Length:** 5 to 12 inches (12.7 to 30.5 cm)
- **Weight:** up to 0.7 pounds (0.3 kg)
- **Lifespan:** up to 7 years
- **Conservation Status:** Least Concern

HABITAT & DIET

These weasels live in a variety of habitats in Asia, Europe, and northern North America. They often choose wooded areas near rivers or marshes. Short-tailed weasels eat mice, voles, shrews, insects, and fish. They also eat leftovers from wolf or bear kills. These weasels store extra food for later.

FAMILY & SOCIAL LIFE

Short-tailed weasels mate in summer. They have up to 18 young the following spring.

FUN FACT

When hunting, a short-tailed weasel will sometimes dance wildly to confuse its prey, giving the weasel a chance to attack.

SNOWSHOE HARE

ALL ABOUT

Snowshoe hares are rusty or grayish brown in summer and white in the winter. The tips of their ears are always black. Snowshoe hares are named for their large hind feet, which enable them to walk easily on snow. Both front and hind feet are covered with thick, stiff fur. Female snowshoe hares are bigger than males.

- **Length:** 16.3 to 20.4 inches (41.4 to 51.8 cm)
- **Weight:** 3.1 to 3.5 pounds (1.4 to 1.6 kg)
- **Lifespan:** up to 5 years
- **Conservation Status:** Least Concern

FUN FACT

Snowshoe hares can swim to escape predators.

HABITAT & DIET

Snowshoe hares live in and around fields, swamps, tundra, and forests in the northern regions of North America. They usually stay near thick vegetation to keep themselves safe. They eat grass, flowers, and new trees and tend to be more active in low light.

FAMILY & SOCIAL LIFE

Both males and females mate with multiple partners during breeding season. Females can have as many as four litters per year, with two to eight babies in each. The young are usually independent within a month of birth.

DID YOU KNOW?

Snowshoe hares take dust baths to remove parasites from their fur.

WOLVERINE

ALL ABOUT

The biggest member of the weasel family, the wolverine is related to otters and ferrets. They are about the size of a medium dog with a face similar to a bear's. Wolverines have sharp claws, powerful jaws, and a thick hide. Flat, wide feet enable them to walk on top of snowpack.

- **Length:** 26 to 41 inches (66 to 104.1 cm)
- **Weight:** up to 66 pounds (29.9 kg)
- **Lifespan:** up to 13 years
- **Conservation Status:** Least Concern

DID YOU KNOW?

Wolverines are nicknamed skunk bears because they release a stinky smell when they are scared.

FUN FACT

Wolverines have been known to walk up to 40 miles (64.4 km) in one day to find food.

HABITAT & DIET

Wolverines live in grasslands, forests, and tundra across the Arctic. They are scavengers, eating whatever is available, mostly carrion. But they are fearless hunters and can kill large animals, including deer. They often fiercely chase other animals away from a meal.

FAMILY & SOCIAL LIFE

Wolverines are generally alone other than while mating. Mothers dig dens deep in the snow. Each litter has two to four kits. They stay in the den with their mother for about 10 weeks.

MUSKRAT

- **About:** Muskrats build dams out of plants. They live in and out of water.
- **Habitat:** marshes, lakes, wooded swamps, streams
- **Conservation Status:** Least Concern

Muskrat

NORTHERN BAT

- **About:** Northern bats eat insects and spiders, which they catch in the air and on surfaces.
- **Habitat:** tree holes or hollows, caves in winter
- **Conservation Status:** Least Concern

Northern Bat

RINGED SEAL

- **About:** This seal spends winter under the sea ice, surfacing through air holes to breathe.
- **Habitat:** Arctic seas
- **Conservation Status:** Least Concern

Ringed Seal

WHITE-BEAKED DOLPHIN

- **About:** These dolphins travel in groups of 5 to 1,500.
- **Habitat:** North Atlantic and Arctic Oceans
- **Conservation Status:** Least Concern

White-beaked dolphin

WRANGEL LEMMING

- **About:** This lemming only lives on a small island near Russia.
- **Habitat:** rocky areas, mountains, tundra
- **Conservation Status:** Data Deficient

Wrangel lemming

BIRDS

Arctic tern

Birds are animals with feathers and wings. Although most birds can fly, some, such as penguins and emus, cannot. Birds are also vertebrates, and they are warm-blooded. They can make their own body heat. All birds have beaks, which are also called bills. Birds reproduce by laying eggs, and their young hatch from these eggs. Sight is a bird's strongest sense.

Birds range in size and appearance. The albatross has a wingspan of 11.5 feet (3.5 m). The heaviest bird is the ostrich, which can weigh up to 300 pounds (136.1 kg). The bee hummingbird is a small bird at only 2.5 inches (6.4 cm) long. It weighs 0.1 ounce (2.8 g).

Birds live all around the world, from tropical forests to Arctic ice and habitats in between. Some birds migrate seasonally. They tend to spend summers in cooler areas and winters in warmer areas.

Atlantic puffin

AMERICAN GOLDEN PLOVER

ALL ABOUT

The fast-flying American golden plover is brownish gray. As it migrates north during the spring, its feathers turn to black and gold.

- **Height:** 9.4 to 11 inches (23.9 to 27.9 cm)
- **Weight:** 4.3 to 6.8 ounces (121.9 to 192.8 g)
- **Lifespan:** 5 to 8 years
- **Conservation Status:** Least Concern

HABITAT & DIET

In the summer, this bird lives in prairies, mudflats, and tundra of Alaska and northern Canada. This plover eats a variety of insects, including beetles, grasshoppers, and flies. It also eats seeds, berries, and snails, as well as crustaceans.

FUN FACT

The American golden plover migrates from the Arctic to South America every winter.

FAMILY & SOCIAL LIFE

Plovers lay eggs in nests in the tundra. After they hatch, the chicks get their own food and begin to fly about three weeks later.

ARCTIC REDPOLL

ALL ABOUT

The Arctic redpoll has light-colored feathers with a patch of red on its head. This bird uses a pouch in its esophagus to store seeds that can be consumed later.

- **Length:** 4.5 to 5.5 inches (11.4 to 14 cm)
- **Weight:** 0.39 to 0.7 ounces (11.1 to 19.8 g)
- **Lifespan:** 4.6 years
- **Conservation Status:** Not Assessed

HABITAT & DIET

The Arctic redpoll lives in the cold, open tundra of northern Canada, Alaska, and Greenland. It eats seeds and parts of trees, shrubs, weeds, and grass. It occasionally eats flies, moths, butterflies, or spiders.

FAMILY & SOCIAL LIFE

Males court females by singing and flying over them. When a female responds, the male brings her food.

DID YOU KNOW?

The Arctic redpoll is also known as the hoary redpoll. Hoarfrost is a type of frost that forms in extreme cold.

ARCTIC SKUA

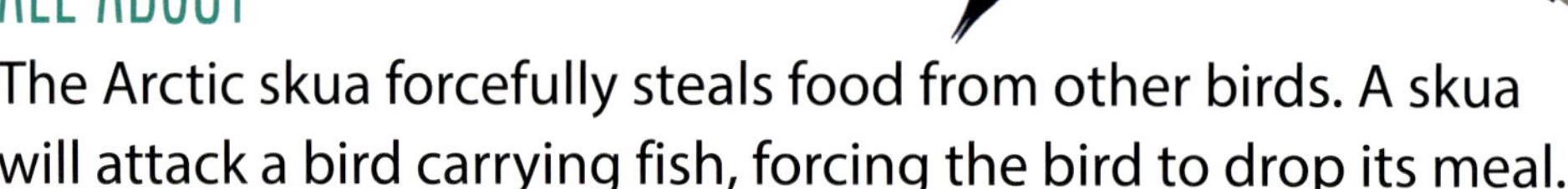

ALL ABOUT

The Arctic skua forcefully steals food from other birds. A skua will attack a bird carrying fish, forcing the bird to drop its meal.

- **Length:** 16 to 18 inches (40.6 to 45.7 cm)
- **Weight:** 12 to 20 ounces (340.2 to 567 g)
- **Lifespan:** 12 to 25 years
- **Conservation Status:** Least Concern

HABITAT & DIET

The Arctic skua mostly lives on the northern Atlantic Ocean, near Norway, Iceland, and Russia. During the winter, it can migrate all the way to the South Pole. The Arctic skua eats fish, insects, small mammals, and birds.

FAMILY & SOCIAL LIFE

While breeding, these birds nest alone or in areas with other Arctic skuas. Otherwise, they sometimes form small groups.

FUN FACT

During breeding season, the Arctic skua grows feather streamers, up to 4.1 inches (10.4 cm) long, from its tail.

ARCTIC TERN

ALL ABOUT

An Arctic tern's round-trip migration, from the Arctic to the Antarctic, is at least 25,000 miles (40,233.6 km) long.

- **Length:** 11 to 16 inches (27.9 to 40.6 cm)
- **Weight:** 3.2 to 4.2 ounces (90.7 to 119.1 g)
- **Lifespan:** 20 to 30 years
- **Conservation Status:** Least Concern

DID YOU KNOW?

The Arctic tern is believed to migrate farther than any other bird.

HABITAT & DIET

Arctic terns dive into ocean water to catch fish and crustaceans. They will steal fish from another bird by surprising it, forcing the bird to drop its food. These terns also eat insects and worms. They live and breed in the Arctic during the summer.

FAMILY & SOCIAL LIFE

Arctic terns look for food in groups and build nests on the ground in larger colonies.

ATLANTIC PUFFIN

ALL ABOUT

When hunting, the Atlantic puffin can dive as deep as 200 feet (61 m).

- **Length:** up to 13.4 inches (34 cm)
- **Weight:** 10.9 to 19.4 ounces (309 to 550 g)
- **Lifespan:** about 20 years
- **Conservation Status:** Vulnerable

HABITAT & DIET

The puffin lives in the North Atlantic Ocean. It catches fish such as herring, sand eels, hake, and capelin. A puffin can hold 10 to 20 fish in its beak at once.

FAMILY & SOCIAL LIFE

Puffins nest in huge colonies of sometimes millions of birds on the coasts of Iceland. The female lays one egg per year in a deep burrow or between rocks.

FUN FACT

A puffin chick is called a puffling.

BARNACLE GOOSE

ALL ABOUT

Barnacle geese fly at about 40.4 miles per hour (65 kmh). They breed on Arctic cliffs.

- **Length:** 25 to 28 inches (63.5 to 71.1 cm)
- **Weight:** 2.2 to 5 pounds (1 to 2.3 kg)
- **Lifespan:** up to 24 years
- **Conservation Status:** Least Concern

DID YOU KNOW?

It was once believed that barnacle geese hatched from barnacles attached to ships.

HABITAT & DIET

Barnacle geese live around Greenland, Norway, and Russia. Many live there year-round. Others migrate to prairies, meadows, mudflats, and marshes in northern Europe. Barnacle geese eat grass or moss.

FAMILY & SOCIAL LIFE

Parents leave the nest soon after the eggs hatch. Their hungry chicks leap from the high cliffs. After they land in the ocean, they swim to shore.

BLACK GUILLEMOT

ALL ABOUT

During breeding season, black guillemots are black with white patches on their wings. In the winter, the plumage on these birds turns grayish white. They spend much of their time swimming and floating on the ocean's surface.

- **Length:** 11.8 to 12.6 inches (30 to 32 cm)
- **Weight:** 0.7 to 1.1 pounds (0.3 to 0.5 kg)
- **Lifespan:** about 11 years
- **Conservation Status:** Least Concern

HABITAT & DIET

Black guillemots are found as far north as the Arctic Circle. They build nests in rocky islands or ocean cliffs, and they sometimes come back to the same nest in later years. They dive for and eat mostly fish. Black guillemots also eat ocean worms, insects, and crustaceans.

DID YOU KNOW?

Black guillemots have bright red legs and feet. The insides of their beaks are red too.

FAMILY & SOCIAL LIFE

A female lays one or two eggs at a time. It can take chicks up to four days to finish hatching. Once the chicks hatch, they climb down to the water. Their parents continue to feed them for up to 50 days before the chicks set out on their own.

BRANT GOOSE

ALL ABOUT

The brant goose is smaller and has a shorter neck than other geese. It has a black head, neck, and chest with white markings on its neck.

- **Length:** 23.3 to 24.5 inches (59.2 to 62.2 cm)
- **Weight:** 2.6 to 3.8 pounds (1.2 to 1.7 kg)
- **Lifespan:** 10 to 20 years
- **Conservation Status:** Least Concern

HABITAT & DIET

Brant geese spend much of their time near shallow bodies of salt water, such as lagoons and marshes. They eat eelgrass, algae, and other saltwater plants while walking along the water's edge. On land, they eat grass and plants. These geese migrate south over the ocean to spend the winters along the Atlantic and Pacific coasts of the United States.

FUN FACT

The oldest Brant goose on record was more than 27 years old.

FAMILY & SOCIAL LIFE

Brant geese group together in large flocks. They spend summers breeding in wetlands in the Arctic regions of northern Canada. They make their nests farther north than any other breed of goose. They lay three to five eggs at a time. The mother keeps them warm and safe until they hatch.

DID YOU KNOW?

Scientists have observed that Brant geese tend to find mates whose white neck markings look similar to their own.

COMMON EIDER

ALL ABOUT

The common eider is the biggest duck in the northern hemisphere.

- **Length:** 23 to 27 inches (58.4 to 68.6 cm)
- **Weight:** 3.3 to 4.3 pounds (1.5 to 2 kg)
- **Lifespan:** 20 years
- **Conservation Status:** Near Threatened

HABITAT & DIET

This duck eats mostly crustaceans and mollusks, especially blue mussels. It catches food by diving underwater and using its bill to pull prey from rocks. It lives and breeds along ocean coasts of northern Canada and Alaska.

FAMILY & SOCIAL LIFE

Eiders line their nests with down feathers. After the eggs hatch, mothers walk the chicks to sea. They often join with other mothers and chicks in a group called a creche.

DID YOU KNOW?

The down feathers of the common eider are considered the softest and warmest. Down gathered from the birds' nests is often used in coats and blankets.

COMMON REDPOLL

ALL ABOUT

The common redpoll is a tiny finch that can survive temperatures as low as –65°F (–53.9°C). In the winter, its insulation feathers increase by about 30 percent. The redpoll sometimes makes tunnels in snow to stay warm.

- **Length:** 5 to 5.5 inches (12.7 to 14 cm)
- **Weight:** 0.4 to 0.6 ounces (11.3 to 17 g)
- **Lifespan:** 2 to 3 years
- **Conservation Status:** Least Concern

FUN FACT

Like the Arctic redpoll, the common redpoll has a crop in its esophagus where it can store food for later.

HABITAT & DIET

Common redpolls live and breed in many areas around the Arctic, but they sometimes fly south to find food. They mostly eat birch seeds but will also eat insects.

FAMILY & SOCIAL LIFE

This little bird usually lays four or five eggs at a time.

GOLDEN EAGLE

ALL ABOUT

One of the largest birds of North America, golden eagles are dark brown with golden feathers on their head and neck. These large raptors build nests usually between 5 and 6 feet (1.5 to 1.8 m) across. Nests are built high in trees or on cliffs, and the eagles enlarge their nests year after year.

- **Length:** up to 33 inches (83.8 cm)
- **Weight:** 7 to 14 pounds (3.2 to 6.4 kg)
- **Lifespan:** 30 years or more
- **Conservation Status:** Least Concern

DID YOU KNOW?

When diving for prey, the golden eagle can fly up to 150 miles per hour (241.4 kmh).

FUN FACT

A golden eagle's nest can be up to 10 feet (3 m) across.

HABITAT & DIET

The golden eagle hunts alone or with its mate over open land such as prairie and tundra. It can be found around the lower regions of the Arctic, especially in Canada and Alaska. It eats smaller animals, often rabbits and squirrels, and occasionally foxes or cranes. Golden eagles that breed in the Arctic migrate south for winter.

FAMILY & SOCIAL LIFE

Golden eagle mates often stay together for several years or more. The female lays one to three eggs at a time, which hatch 41 to 45 days later. Chicks stay with their parents for nearly three months.

GREAT BLACK-BACKED GULL

ALL ABOUT

The great black-backed gull has a dark back and wings. It also has a large white head and a yellow beak.

- **Length:** 25 to 32 inches (63.5 to 81.3 cm)
- **Weight:** 1.7 to 5.1 pounds (0.8 to 2.3 kg)
- **Lifespan:** 10 to 20 years
- **Conservation Status:** Least Concern

HABITAT & DIET

This gull is not a picky eater. It steals food from other birds and will also eat chicks and eggs. It sometimes forages through trash for human food and will eat carrion. This bird's diet also includes fish, worms, insects, berries, and crustaceans.

The great black-backed gull can be found along ocean coastlines and inland lakes of northern Europe, Greenland, and northern regions of North America. Winter migration takes the gulls south, but not much farther than southern parts of the United States.

FAMILY & SOCIAL LIFE

The great black-backed gull builds nests on the ground or on ocean cliffs. The female lays two to three eggs at a time. Both parents care for the eggs and feed the chicks after they hatch. Chicks stay with their parents until they learn to fly, at about seven weeks old. Some stay a little longer.

FUN FACT

The great black-backed gull is the biggest gull in the world.

GYRFALCON

ALL ABOUT

The gyrfalcon is a hunter. Some gyrfalcons are gray, and others are white with darker gray speckles. Females can be almost twice as big as males.

- **Length:** 18.9 to 25.2 inches (48 to 64 cm)
- **Weight:** 3.1 to 4.6 pounds (1.4 to 2.1 kg)
- **Lifespan:** 12 to 15 years
- **Conservation Status:** Least Concern

DID YOU KNOW?

During the Middle Ages, kings preferred to use gyrfalcons in falconry, a sport in which falcons are used to aid in hunting.

HABITAT & DIET

The largest falcon in the world, this bird lives mostly in and around the Arctic Circle. Some travel south for winter, but not far. The gyrfalcon hunts small birds, especially ptarmigans, and medium-sized birds like geese and seabirds. The gyrfalcon also eats hares, fox pups, and lemmings.

FAMILY & SOCIAL LIFE

The gyrfalcon lives by itself outside of mating season. It usually builds its nest on a cliff. But it sometimes uses an abandoned raven's or eagle's nest in a tree. Gyrfalcons often return to the same nests for many years. Before the spring thaw, the female lays three to five eggs. Once hatched, the chicks start flying between six and eight weeks of age.

FUN FACT

During a dive, the gyrfalcon can fly up to 130 miles per hour (209.2 kmh).

HUDSONIAN GODWIT

ALL ABOUT

The Hudsonian godwit is a sandpiper that breeds in the northern parts of Canada and Alaska. It migrates to Argentina and Chile for the winter, traveling up to 16,000 miles (25,749.5 km) round trip.

- **Length:** 14.2 to 16.5 inches (36.1 to 41.9 cm)
- **Weight:** 6.9 to 12.6 ounces (195.6 to 357.2 g)
- **Lifespan:** 10 to 12 years
- **Conservation Status:** Least Concern

FUN FACT

The Hudsonian godwit can fly for an entire week without stopping.

HABITAT & DIET

The Hudsonian godwit forages through shallow water and uses its long thin beak to dig for food in the mud. During migration, this bird eats crustaceans, sea worms, and mollusks.

FAMILY & SOCIAL LIFE

The Hudsonian godwit builds a hidden nest in a mudflat, then usually lays four eggs. Only about one in four of the chicks survive.

IVORY GULL

ALL ABOUT

The ivory gull has all white feathers. It spends most of its time on sea ice in the far northern areas of the Arctic. Melting sea ice puts this gull at risk, and its population has decreased in the last decades.

- **Length:** 15.8 to 17 inches (40.1 to 43.2 cm)
- **Weight:** 1 to 1.5 pounds (0.5 to 0.7 kg)
- **Lifespan:** 8 to 17 years
- **Conservation Status:** Near Threatened

HABITAT & DIET

The ivory gull is a scavenger, eating carrion, scat, and remains from polar bear kills. It also eats fish and invertebrates.

FAMILY & SOCIAL LIFE

The ivory gull makes nests from seaweed and mud on cliffs, flat rocky ground, or occasionally on floating ice packs.

DID YOU KNOW?

Red is a color that ivory gulls tend to notice. This most likely helps them find blood of carrion, and their next meal.

KING EIDER

ALL ABOUT

The king eider's scientific name, *Somateria spectabilis*, comes from two phrases. One means "body wool," for the bird's warm feathers. The other means "remarkable display," for the male's brightly colored plumage during mating season. Females are brown and able to blend in well with their surroundings.

- **Length:** 18 to 25 inches (45.7 to 63.5 cm)
- **Weight:** 2.6 to 4.6 pounds (1.2 to 2.1 kg)
- **Lifespan:** 15 to 20 years
- **Conservation Status:** Least Concern

DID YOU KNOW?

The king eider has the shortest incubation time of any water bird, at 22 to 24 days.

FUN FACT

A king eider can dive deep underwater, sometimes more than 100 feet (30.5 m).

HABITAT & DIET

The king eider eats mostly mollusks but also crustaceans and insects. It also eats plants, including algae and eelgrass. It spends breeding season in the tundra, near coasts or lakes all around the Arctic. In the winter, it stays on the ocean or along the coasts.

FAMILY & SOCIAL LIFE

The female uses grass and down from her body to build a nest. She lays four or five eggs and then cares for them for just over three weeks. Once they hatch, several mothers gather to care for their young together.

LITTLE AUK

ALL ABOUT

The little auk, sometimes called a dovekie, is a small black-and-white seabird. In the summer, its head is all black, and in the winter, the underside of its head turns white. It can fly as fast as 43.5 miles per hour (70 kmh).

- **Length:** 7.5 to 9.1 inches (19.1 to 23.1 cm)
- **Weight:** 4.7 to 7.2 ounces (133.2 to 204.1 g)
- **Lifespan:** 10 to 25 years
- **Conservation Status:** Least Concern

HABITAT & DIET

Little auks dive in a zigzag pattern, as deep as 100 feet (30.5 m) below the water's surface. Then on the way back up, they catch small fish and crustaceans. When these birds aren't breeding, they spend their time on the ocean near northern Europe, northeastern North America, and Greenland.

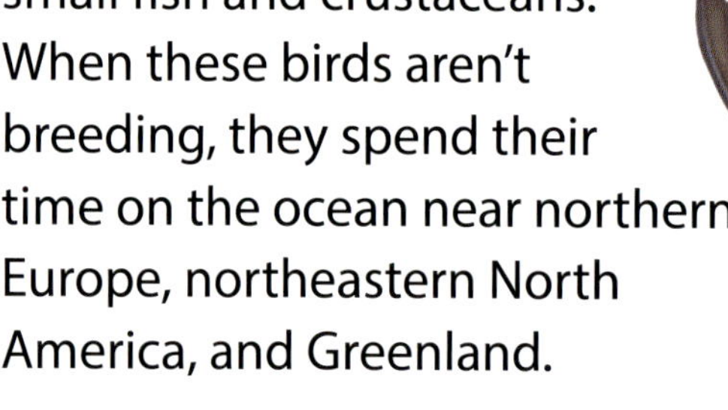

DID YOU KNOW?

In breeding colonies, little auks make a variety of sounds, including trilling and clucking.

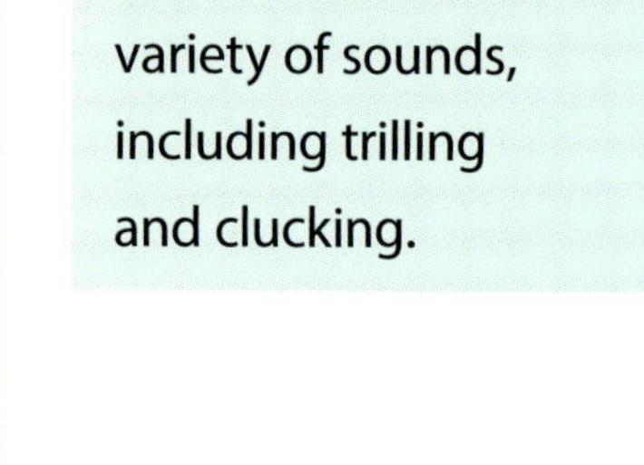

FAMILY & SOCIAL LIFE

These birds gather in huge flocks of up to a million birds. During their summer breeding season, they lay their eggs on rocky cliffs. The female lays one blue egg at a time. After hatching, the chicks stay in the nest for four weeks. Most chicks in the colony leave within a couple days of one another.

FUN FACT

The little auk stores food for its young in a pouch under its beak.

LONG-TAILED JAEGER

ALL ABOUT

The long-tailed jaeger (pronounced YAY-gur) spends most of its time over the ocean, often following fishing boats. In some places, jaegers are called skuas.

- **Length:** 15 to 24.8 inches (38.1 to 63 cm)
- **Weight:** 7.7 to 12.1 ounces (218.3 to 343 g)
- **Lifespan:** 8 to 9 years
- **Conservation Status:** Least Concern

HABITAT & DIET

The long-tailed jaeger is a hunter. It swoops down from the sky to catch lemmings and other rodents, as well as fish. Sometimes it steals food from other birds. During its breeding season, it can be found in many areas across the dry Arctic tundra. Other times, it lives on the ocean, far from land.

FUN FACT

The long-tailed jaeger is more likely to have young during years when the lemming population is high.

FAMILY & SOCIAL LIFE

During spring mating season, males court females by displaying their flying skills, which include many zigzags. Multiple males will perform for one female. The nest of a long-tailed jaeger is a small indentation on the ground. Females lay two eggs, and both parents take turns incubating. They use one foot to hold an egg against their body for warmth.

DID YOU KNOW?

During mating season, the tails of male jaegers are 5 to 10 inches (12.7 to 25.4 cm) longer than during other times of year.

LOON

ALL ABOUT

The loon, which is also known as the great northern diver, is a large water bird. During the winter, its feathers are gray and white. But when breeding, this bird has a black head and neck and distinct black-and-white patterning. This bird is also known for its red eyes.

- **Length:** 26 to 35.8 inches (66 to 90.9 cm)
- **Weight:** 5.5 to 13.5 pounds (2.5 to 6.1 kg)
- **Lifespan:** up to 28 years
- **Conservation Status:** Least Concern

DID YOU KNOW?

Although most birds have hollow bones, the loon has several solid, heavier bones. The weight aids in diving, but it also makes taking off in flight challenging.

HABITAT & DIET

In the summer, the loon spends most of its time on freshwater lakes in Greenland, Iceland, and the northern regions of North America. It uses its large feet to dive underwater, catching fish, shrimp, leeches, and plants.

FAMILY & SOCIAL LIFE

The male and female work together to dig a nest in dirt or living plants. Then the female lays one to three eggs. After the eggs hatch, the parents carry the chicks on their backs to keep them safe. Chicks start diving two days after they hatch.

NORTHERN FULMAR

ALL ABOUT

The northern fulmar mostly lives at sea in cold waters of the North Atlantic and Arctic Oceans. This gray-and-white bird produces a stinky oil in its stomach, which it spits at predators.

- **Length:** 15.3 to 19.7 inches (38.9 to 50 cm)
- **Weight:** 1 to 2.2 pounds (0.5 to 1 kg)
- **Lifespan:** 30 years
- **Conservation Status:** Least Concern

HABITAT & DIET

The northern fulmar eats carrion, shrimp, squid, fish, and jellyfish. It will sometimes trail fishing boats to scavenge scraps.

FAMILY & SOCIAL LIFE

This bird breeds on high cliffs, often using the same nest for many years. Females lay one egg at a time. Both parents incubate the egg and care for their chick once hatched.

DID YOU KNOW?

The northern fulmar's name comes from old Norse words meaning *foul gull.*

NORTHERN GANNET

ALL ABOUT

From about 100 feet (30.5 m) above the ocean, the northern gannet dives straight into the water at up to 60 miles per hour (96.6 kmh). This bird has excellent vision, even underwater.

- **Length:** 36.4 to 43.3 inches (92.5 to 110 cm)
- **Weight:** 5.3 to 7.9 pounds (2.4 to 3.6 kg)
- **Lifespan:** 17 years
- **Conservation Status:** Least Concern

FUN FACT

Northern gannets have been returning to some nesting areas for hundreds of years.

HABITAT & DIET

The northern gannet lives and hunts in the North Atlantic Ocean. It usually swallows its fish before coming back to the surface. It sometimes follows fishing boats or steals from other birds.

FAMILY & SOCIAL LIFE

Northern gannets nest on rocky cliffs and ledges. Colonies can have thousands of nests.

PINK-FOOTED GOOSE

ALL ABOUT

The pink-footed goose is a small goose with pink legs, feet, and beak. Its body is mostly gray brown with white under its tail.

- **Length:** 24 to 30 inches (61 to 76.2 cm)
- **Weight:** 4.2 to 8.5 pounds (1.9 to 3.9 kg)
- **Lifespan:** 22 years
- **Conservation Status:** Least Concern

HABITAT & DIET

Most of these geese spend summer breeding season in Iceland and Greenland. They are social birds who nest and travel in flocks of thousands. They usually migrate to Europe in the winter, but they have occasionally been seen in Canada. They eat grass, root vegetables, and grains, which they find while walking through farms and grasslands.

FAMILY & SOCIAL LIFE

These geese make nests in shallow depressions, adding plants and down. When chicks are 10 to 20 days old, their parents molt. Then neither the parents nor the chicks can fly. They walk together until the adults' feathers come back in and the chicks learn to fly. Goose chicks are called goslings.

DID YOU KNOW?

Before the chicks learn to fly, pink-footed goose families can walk up to 15 miles (24.1 km) across the tundra.

RAVEN

ALL ABOUT

The raven's body is completely black, including its beak, eyes, legs, and feet. It is bigger than most songbirds. The raven is thought to be one of the most intelligent birds. It makes more than 30 different sounds.

- **Length:** 22.1 to 27.2 inches (56.1 to 69.1 cm)
- **Weight:** 1.5 to 3.6 pounds (0.7 to 1.6 kg)
- **Lifespan:** 6 to 13 years
- **Conservation Status:** Least Concern

FUN FACT

Ravens have been part of many cultural mythologies.

HABITAT & DIET

This bird is an omnivore. It eats insects, grains, rodents, and other birds' eggs. It also eats decaying animals, the insects that feed on them, trash, and feces. The raven can live in a variety of environments, from hot deserts to frozen tundra. It seems to prefer forests, but it also spends time in prairies.

FAMILY & SOCIAL LIFE

Ravens are mostly solitary, spending time alone or with one other raven. Ravens build large nests, up to 5 feet (1.5 m) across, out of sticks, tree bark, and hair. Their nests are built high on cliffs or treetops.

DID YOU KNOW?

Ravens will perform acrobatics such as diving or flying upside down. These actions are thought to be a form of play.

RAZORBILL

ALL ABOUT

The razorbill is a seabird that lives in large colonies on cliffs near the northern Atlantic Ocean. During breeding season, an adult razorbill is black with a white belly and has distinct white stripes. When this bird is not breeding, the feathers on its face and neck turn white.

- **Length:** 16.9 inches (42.9 cm)
- **Weight:** 17.8 to 31.4 ounces (504.6 to 890.2 g)
- **Lifespan:** 13 years
- **Conservation Status:** Least Concern

DID YOU KNOW?

Razorbills can dive more than 300 feet (91.4 m) below the ocean's surface to hunt for food.

FUN FACT

The inside of the razorbill's mouth is bright yellow.

HABITAT & DIET

The razorbill dives underwater to catch fish such as herring, sand lances, sticklebacks, and cod. Sometimes this bird eats marine worms and crustaceans or steals fish from other birds.

FAMILY & SOCIAL LIFE

Razorbills build nests from grass and small rocks on cliff ledges. They sometimes use old rabbit or puffin nests. Females lay a single egg. After the chick hatches, both parents feed it fish. At about 20 days old, the chick jumps off the cliff to the ocean. This leap can be hundreds of feet long.

RED PHALAROPE

ALL ABOUT

The red phalarope has a reddish-orange neck and body with a black-and-white head and wings. When not breeding, it is gray and white. In Europe, this bird is known as the gray phalarope.

- **Length:** 7.9 to 8.7 inches (20.1 to 22.1 cm)
- **Weight:** 1.5 to 2.1 ounces (42.5 to 59.5 g)
- **Lifespan:** 8 to 10 years
- **Conservation Status:** Least Concern

HABITAT & DIET

In the summer, the red phalarope builds nests along the coasts of Arctic tundra. To find food, this bird swims in small circles. This creates a whirlpool that pulls up insects and invertebrates. The red phalarope migrates south to spend the winter on the ocean.

FUN FACT

Female red phalaropes are larger than males and have brighter feathers during mating season.

DID YOU KNOW?

Red phalaropes are often seen with pods of whales as they all feed on fish brought to the ocean's surface by upwellings.

FAMILY & SOCIAL LIFE

During a breeding season, the female red phalarope often lays two clutches of eggs with two different mates. Each clutch has two to four eggs. After she lays eggs, the male of each clutch cares for the eggs and keeps them warm until they hatch. Then he walks the chicks to water. They stay together for a few days.

FUN FACT

Red-throated loons sometimes fish in flocks. When a school of fish is spotted, the flock dives down for a meal together.

RED-THROATED LOON/RED-THROATED DIVER

ALL ABOUT

Red-throated loons are a small type of loon. They are known for the reddish-brown patch on their neck that appears during summer breeding season. They have red eyes and a gray head. In the winter, their neck patch disappears, and their coloring lightens to white and gray.

- **Length:** 22.1 to 26.8 inches (56.1 to 68.1 cm)
- **Weight:** 2.8 to 5.4 pounds (1.3 to 2.4 kg)
- **Lifespan:** 20 years
- **Conservation Status:** Least Concern

HABITAT & DIET

Red-throated loons live and breed in the Arctic tundra in lakes and ponds. They catch fish by diving, both while swimming and from the air. They spend winters along ocean coastlines.

FAMILY & SOCIAL LIFE

Red-throated loons migrate alone or in small groups of five or six birds. They tend to mate for life, and females usually lay two eggs at a time. Both parents build and defend the nest. Chicks start swimming about one day after hatching.

DID YOU KNOW?

The red-throated loon swallows pebbles to help digest food. An organ called a gizzard uses them to grind food.

ROCK PTARMIGAN

ALL ABOUT

The small rock ptarmigan has distinct red eyebrows. It is sometimes called a snow chicken for its white winter feathers, which help it camouflage. During the summer, its feathers change to a speckled brown.

- **Length:** 12.6 to 15.8 inches (32 to 40.1 cm)
- **Weight:** 15.5 to 22.6 ounces (439.4 to 640.7 g)
- **Lifespan:** 2 to 4 years
- **Conservation Status:** Least Concern

HABITAT & DIET

This bird nests in high, dry tundra in Arctic and alpine areas. They eat mostly plants, including leaves, berries, seeds, and flowers. But they also eat insects, spiders, and snails. In the winter, they occasionally follow caribou or musk oxen, which scrape snow off the ground, revealing food for the birds.

FUN FACT

The name *ptarmigan* comes from a Gaelic word meaning "croaker."

FAMILY & SOCIAL LIFE

Males are hostile toward one another during mating season. They claim territories by performing an elaborate flight while singing. Females walk through the breeding grounds to choose a mate, and the males perform another song and dance. After mating, the female lays between 3 and 13 eggs.

DID YOU KNOW?

Rock ptarmigans have feathers on their feet and legs, which help the birds walk on snow and keep them warm.

ROCK SANDPIPER

ALL ABOUT

The rock sandpiper has a long, pointy beak, used for finding food in small rock crevices.

- **Length:** 7.1 to 9.4 inches (18 to 23.9 cm)
- **Weight:** 2 to 4.6 ounces (56.7 to 130.4 g)
- **Lifespan:** 7 years
- **Conservation Status:** Least Concern

DID YOU KNOW?

To distract predators, rock sandpiper parents will sometimes pretend to have a broken wing while flying.

HABITAT & DIET

This bird spends the winter on rocky coastlines around Alaska and Russia. It spends summer breeding season in Arctic tundra. The rock sandpiper pokes its beak into mud to find worms and clams. It also uses its beak to hammer open mollusks. Other food sources include berries, moss, and seeds.

FAMILY & SOCIAL LIFE

The rock sandpiper lays about four eggs at a time. Both parents care for the eggs.

ROUGH-LEGGED BUZZARD

ALL ABOUT

The rough-legged buzzard, also called a rough-legged hawk, got its name from its heavily feathered legs and feet. This bird can be found in Arctic regions of North America and Eurasia.

- **Length:** 18.5 to 20.5 inches (47 to 52.1 cm)
- **Weight:** 1.6 to 3.1 pounds (0.7 to 1.4 kg)
- **Lifespan:** up to 18 years
- **Conservation Status:** Least Concern

FUN FACT

More rough-legged buzzards breed when the population of rodents, the birds' main food source, is high.

HABITAT & DIET

This hunter hovers in the air before swooping down to catch small animals such as voles, rabbits, and lemmings. It also eats birds, insects, and decaying animals. It breeds in open tundra areas and travels south for the winter.

FAMILY & SOCIAL LIFE

The rough-legged buzzard nests on cliffs, usually laying three to six eggs at a time. At 16 days, nestlings can swallow lemmings whole.

RUDDY TURNSTONE

ALL ABOUT

The ruddy turnstone has patterning similar to a calico cat's. The bird's spiny feet and short, sharp toenails prevent it from slipping on wet rocks.

- **Length:** 6.3 to 8.3 inches (16 to 21.1 cm)
- **Weight:** 3 to 6.7 ounces (85 to 189.9 g)
- **Lifespan:** 6 to 7 years
- **Conservation Status:** Least Concern

HABITAT & DIET

This bird breeds in areas across the Arctic tundra and winters along coastlines. It flips rocks and shells with its beak to find insects and crustaceans for food. Sometimes it eats other birds' eggs, as well as carrion, small fish, berries, moss, and seeds.

FAMILY & SOCIAL LIFE

Ruddy turnstone chicks are left by their parents to migrate with other chicks to their winter habitat, often thousands of miles away.

FUN FACT

Ruddy turnstones travel from the Arctic to as far away as Australia during the winter.

SANDERLING

ALL ABOUT

A type of sandpiper, the sanderling can be found in the Arctic tundra of Alaska and northern Canada during the summer. Unlike most sandpipers, the sanderling doesn't have a back toe, enabling it to run fast.

- **Length:** 7 to 8 inches (17.8 to 20.3 cm)
- **Weight:** 1.4 to 3.5 ounces (39.7 to 99.2 g)
- **Lifespan:** 7 years
- **Conservation Status:** Least Concern

DID YOU KNOW?

Nonbreeding sanderlings don't migrate north in the spring and instead stay on beaches farther south.

HABITAT & DIET

During the winter, sanderlings live along the coast. As waves recede, the birds pluck mollusks, crustaceans, worms, and insects from the sand.

FAMILY & SOCIAL LIFE

Sanderlings gather in groups to protect themselves from predators. They often fly and sleep together in tight flocks.

SANDHILL CRANE

ALL ABOUT

Sandhill cranes are tall, mostly gray birds with a long neck, beak, and legs. Adults have a red spot on their head. Sandhill cranes can be found in Alaska and Canada during their summer breeding season.

- **Length:** 47.2 inches (119.9 cm)
- **Weight:** 7.5 to 10.8 pounds (3.4 to 4.9 kg)
- **Lifespan:** 20 to 30 years
- **Conservation Status:** Least Concern

HABITAT & DIET

The sandhill crane eats grains and invertebrates. It finds food by walking through marshes, farmland, and grasslands. This bird's diet also consists of plant roots, rodents, frogs, berries, and lizards.

FUN FACT

The oldest sandhill crane fossil ever found is thought to be 2.5 million years old.

DID YOU KNOW?

Some sandhill cranes stay farther south in Florida and Mississippi, even during breeding season.

FAMILY & SOCIAL LIFE

Sandhill cranes migrate south and spend winter in huge flocks of sometimes tens of thousands of birds. They can travel as many as 400 miles (643.7 km) in a day. These birds court one another with elaborate dances in which they jump and flap their wings while making sounds.

After hatching, chicks leave their nests and are able to swim within 8 hours. But chicks will continue to stay near their parents for 9 or 10 months.

SNOW BUNTING

ALL ABOUT

The snow bunting's white color and warm leg feathers help it survive in its Arctic environment.

- **Length:** 5.9 inches (15 cm)
- **Weight:** 1.1 to 1.6 ounces (31.2 to 45.4 g)
- **Lifespan:** 6 to 9 years
- **Conservation Status:** Least Concern

HABITAT & DIET

Snow buntings search the ground for food, such as seeds, plant buds, insects, and crustaceans. The birds nest in rocky Arctic areas of northern Canada and Alaska and spend summer farther south in open areas such as prairies and lake shores.

FAMILY & SOCIAL LIFE

Male snow buntings migrate north ahead of females to find good nesting sites. When females arrive a few weeks later, males court them with flying acrobatics.

FUN FACT

Snow buntings are sometimes called snowflakes.

SNOW GOOSE

ALL ABOUT

The snow goose is mostly white, with black on its wingtips. Some have a gray body and wings. But these "blue geese" are the same breed.

- **Length:** 27.2 to 32.7 inches (69.1 to 83.1 cm)
- **Weight:** 3.5 to 7.3 pounds (1.6 to 3.3 kg)
- **Lifespan:** 19 to 26 years
- **Conservation Status:** Least Concern

HABITAT & DIET

The snow goose pulls up and eats wild plants and farm crops. During the spring, these birds migrate to the Arctic tundra, mostly of northern Canada, to breed.

DID YOU KNOW?

A snow goose can poop between 6 and 15 times per hour. Food moves through its digestive tract quickly.

FAMILY & SOCIAL LIFE

Snow geese travel in large flocks that range from a few dozen to hundreds of thousands. They usually lay three to five eggs. When the eggs hatch, the family walks together to find food.

SNOWY OWL

ALL ABOUT

Snowy owls are mostly white with yellow eyes and feathered legs. Young owls and adult females have brown- or black-patterned feathers. Snowy owls are most active during the day. But in the long daylight hours of Arctic summer, they'll hunt any time.

- **Length:** 20.5 to 27.9 inches (52.1 to 70.9 cm)
- **Weight:** 3.5 to 6.5 pounds (1.6 to 2.9 kg)
- **Lifespan:** 10 to 17 years
- **Conservation Status:** Vulnerable

HABITAT & DIET

Snowy owls live in open areas with few trees. They fly close to the ground. They can be found north of the Arctic Circle during the summer, though some will stay in the region throughout the year.

A snowy owl mostly eats lemmings, sometimes consuming more than 1,600 in a year. It also eats birds, other mammals, and fish. To hunt, the snowy owl stays still, listening and watching for hours at a time.

FAMILY & SOCIAL LIFE

The snowy owl can lay between 3 and 11 eggs. When the lemming population is high, snowy owls can have two or three times as many chicks.

DID YOU KNOW?

Snowy owls can't move their eyes. They can turn their head far enough to see behind them.

THICK-BILLED MURRE

ALL ABOUT

The thick-billed murre has a black head, neck, and back. The tops of its wings are also black, and the rest of its body is white and gray.

- **Length:** 17.7 inches (45 cm)
- **Weight:** 1.6 to 3.3 pounds (0.7 to 1.5 kg)
- **Lifespan:** up to 25 years
- **Conservation Status:** Least Concern

HABITAT & DIET

When not breeding, the thick-billed murre lives in the open ocean of the high Arctic. It dives deep under the water to catch fish, squid, and crustaceans.

FUN FACT

The thick-billed murre can fly up to 75 miles per hour (120.7 kmh).

FAMILY & SOCIAL LIFE

The thick-billed murre nests in large groups along cliff edges. The female lays one egg. Then she uses small rocks and feces to build a short wall around the egg to prevent it from rolling off. The chicks hatch in 30 to 35 days. After three weeks, chicks and parents migrate to the open ocean. They begin with a long swim, up to 620 miles (997.8 km). This is unusual for birds, most of which migrate by flying.

DID YOU KNOW?

The thick-billed murre often dives deeper than 330 feet (100.6 m) to catch prey. It is one of the deepest-diving birds.

TUNDRA SWAN

ALL ABOUT

The tundra swan is white with black legs and feet. It can fly up to 50 miles per hour (80.5 kmh).

- **Length:** 47.2 to 57.9 inches (119.9 to 147.1 cm)
- **Weight:** 8.4 to 23.2 pounds (3.8 to 10.5 kg)
- **Lifespan:** 16 to 24 years
- **Conservation Status:** Least Concern

DID YOU KNOW?

The tundra swan is nicknamed the whistling swan for the sound its wings make while flying.

HABITAT & DIET

The tundra swan lives along ocean coastlines or on lakes or estuaries of the Arctic regions of North America. In the winter, it lives on tundra lakes and ponds. It eats algae, pondweed, other water plants, and invertebrates.

FAMILY & SOCIAL LIFE

Tundra swans migrate in flocks of a hundred or more. A female lays three to five eggs in a nest made of plant material.

WHITE-TAILED EAGLE

FUN FACT

The white-tailed eagle's tail doesn't turn white until the bird is eight years old.

ALL ABOUT

The white-tailed eagle is a large bird of prey that often lives near the sea. Its wingspan can be up to 8 feet (2.4 m) across.

- **Length:** 29 to 36 inches (73.7 to 91.4 cm)
- **Weight:** 6.8 to 15.2 pounds (3.1 to 6.9 kg)
- **Lifespan:** up to 30 years
- **Conservation Status:** Least Concern

HABITAT & DIET

The white-tailed eagle lives in a variety of Arctic areas including Greenland, northern Russia, and Norway. It eats fish, ducks, gulls, muskrats, hares, and carrion. It sometimes steals food from other raptors.

FAMILY & SOCIAL LIFE

The female lays two white eggs in a large nest built high in trees or on a cliff. The chicks are born featherless.

ADDITIONAL BIRDS

Arctic peregrine falcon

ARCTIC PEREGRINE FALCON

- **About:** It is estimated that this bird can dive more than 200 miles per hour (321.9 kmh).
- **Habitat:** Arctic tundra
- **Conservation Status:** Least Concern

Glaucous gull

GLAUCOUS GULL

- **About:** This large gull eats almost anything, including carrion, insects, fruit, eggs, and trash.
- **Habitat:** cliffs, ocean shorelines
- **Conservation Status:** Least Concern

Harlequin duck

HARLEQUIN DUCK

- **About:** This duck is nicknamed the sea mouse due to the squeaking noise it makes.
- **Habitat:** rivers and streams, rocky coastlines
- **Conservation Status:** Least Concern

LAPLAND LONGSPUR

- **About:** This songbird can eat between 3,000 and 10,000 insects and seeds in a day.
- **Habitat:** tundra grasslands
- **Conservation Status:** Least Concern

Lapland longspur

Northern pintail

NORTHERN PINTAIL

- **About:** Northern pintails use their beak to collect insects and seeds from the water's surface.
- **Habitat:** wetlands, prairies, grasslands, ponds, lakes
- **Conservation Status:** Least Concern

WESTERN SIBERIAN EAGLE OWL

- **About:** This bird's vocalizations include barks and growls.
- **Habitat:** rocky, mountainous areas
- **Conservation Status:** Least Concern

Western Siberian eagle owl

FISH

Fish are a diverse group of aquatic vertebrates. They live in salt or fresh water and at a variety of depths and environments. Their habitats include rivers, ponds, lakes, deep oceans, shallow coastlines, and estuaries. Fish eat a variety of foods, including plants, small invertebrates, and other fish.

Most fish are cold-blooded, and most hatch from eggs. Fish larvae sometimes live in different habitats and eat different foods than adults. Fish usually have gill slits and tails for at least part of their lives.

Arctic char

Shorthorn sculpin

Fish are not all the same. Bony fish include seahorses, sunfishes, and marlin. Fish made of cartilage include rays, skates, and sharks. Jawless fish, such as lampreys and hagfish, often use suction to feed.

Fish species have been on Earth for 450 million years.

FUN FACT

The shorthorn sculpin sometimes makes grunting sounds in the water.

ARCTIC CHAR

ALL ABOUT

The Arctic char spends most of its time in water below 55°F (12.8°C). If surface water is warmer, char tend to swim deeper.

- **Length:** 6 to 38 inches (15.2 to 96.5 cm)
- **Weight:** 2 to 15 pounds (0.9 to 6.8 kg)
- **Lifespan:** 15 to 20 years
- **Conservation Status:** Least Concern

HABITAT & DIET

The Arctic char mostly lives in the Arctic Ocean, but it swims into freshwater lakes and rivers to breed. This char eats smaller fish, insects, crustaceans, mollusks, and plankton.

FAMILY & SOCIAL LIFE

An adult Arctic char usually spawns every other fall. The female lays eggs in a nest she digs in gravel at the bottom of a lake. The eggs hatch about two months later.

DID YOU KNOW?

During spawning season, the belly of the male Arctic char turns orange, yellow, and gold.

ARCTIC GRAYLING

ALL ABOUT

The Arctic grayling has a large red-tipped fin on its back. This fin often has red, blue, or purple markings.

- **Length:** 8 to 30 inches (20.3 to 76.2 cm)
- **Weight:** 5 to 8 pounds (2.3 to 3.6 kg)
- **Lifespan:** 5 to 32 years
- **Conservation Status:** Least Concern

HABITAT & DIET

Some Arctic graylings live in lakes or ponds, whereas others live in rivers. The Arctic grayling mostly eats water insects, but it also eats crustaceans and zooplankton. Small fish and fish eggs are also part of its diet.

FAMILY & SOCIAL LIFE

Arctic graylings spawn in springtime. A female lays her eggs, between 1,500 and 30,000 at a time, on gravel at the bottom of streams.

FUN FACT

The Arctic grayling is a member of the salmon family.

ARCTIC SHANNY

ALL ABOUT

The Arctic shanny is a small ray-finned fish, a group of fish with fins that fan out in a ray. The Arctic shanny has an elongated body and a dorsal fin that runs along most of its back.

- **Length:** 8.7 inches (22.1 cm)
- **Weight:** up to 0.5 ounces (14.2 g)
- **Lifespan:** 2 to 6 years
- **Conservation Status:** Secure

HABITAT & DIET

This fish can be found in shallow sandy and rocky areas of the Arctic, the northern Pacific, and the northwestern Atlantic Oceans. It eats copepods, a type of crustacean, as well as worms.

FAMILY & SOCIAL LIFE

The Arctic shanny spawns in the winter. This fish tends to be solitary.

FUN FACT

The Arctic shanny has 40 to 46 spines along its dorsal fin.

COD

ALL ABOUT

Two types of cod that live in the Arctic are the Greenland cod and the saffron cod. The Greenland cod has three fins on its back and two on the bottom of its body. The saffron cod is a dark olive color with silvery sides. Its upper jaw extends from its face.

- **Length:** 13.8 to 31.5 inches (35.1 to 80 cm)
- **Weight:** up to 201 pounds (91.2 kg)
- **Lifespan:** 9 to 21 years
- **Conservation Status:** Not Assessed

HABITAT & DIET

The Greenland cod usually swims near the ocean bottom in cold Arctic waters near shorelines. At times, these cods eat one another. The saffron cod usually lives in the upper 75 feet (22.9 m) of the western Arctic Ocean and Bering Sea. It swims toward the shore under sea ice for its winter mating season. Both types of cod eat worms, crustaceans, and fish.

Greenland cod

FUN FACT

Greenland cod are also known as *ogac*, a name given by the Inuktitut people.

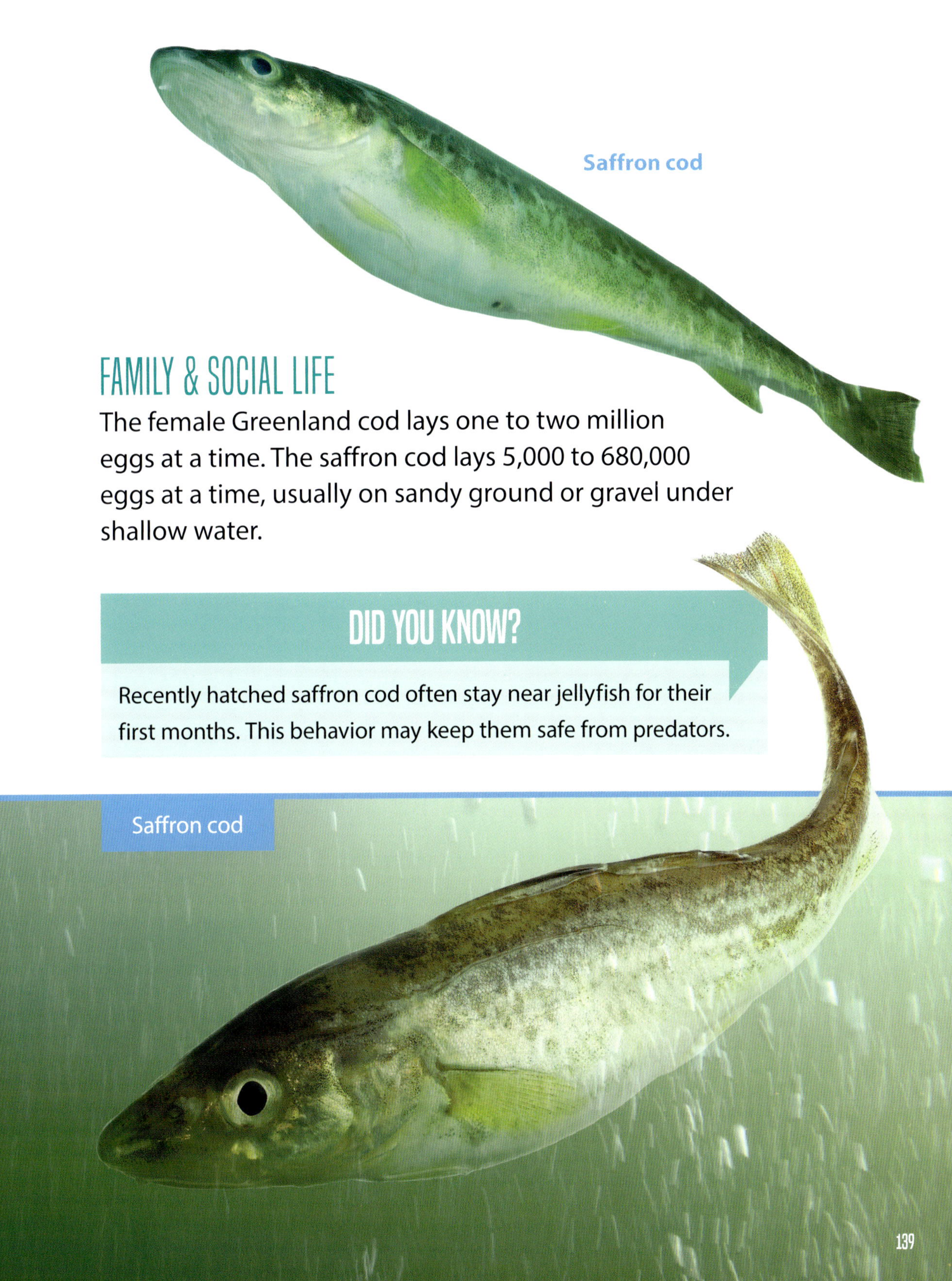

Saffron cod

FAMILY & SOCIAL LIFE

The female Greenland cod lays one to two million eggs at a time. The saffron cod lays 5,000 to 680,000 eggs at a time, usually on sandy ground or gravel under shallow water.

DID YOU KNOW?

Recently hatched saffron cod often stay near jellyfish for their first months. This behavior may keep them safe from predators.

Saffron cod

GREENLAND SHARK

ALL ABOUT

The Greenland shark is a large, slow-moving creature. It lives longer than any other vertebrate on Earth.

- **Length:** 8 to 23 feet (2.4 to 7 m)
- **Weight:** up to 1.5 tons (1.4 mt)
- **Lifespan:** about 400 years
- **Conservation Status:** Vulnerable

FUN FACT

The Greenland shark is the only known shark species that can survive the cold Arctic waters all year long.

HABITAT & DIET

The shark lives in deep, cold water, mostly in the Arctic Ocean and North Atlantic Ocean. It eats many kinds of fish, including eels, flounders, sculpin, and sharks. It also eats crustaceans, birds, and carrion.

FAMILY & SOCIAL LIFE

Females are able to reproduce once they're 13 feet (4 m) long, when they're about 150 years old. Up to 10 eggs at a time stay inside the female's body until they hatch.

LAKE TROUT

ALL ABOUT

The lake trout is not a trout but, rather, a type of char fish. Yet the lake trout has a body similar to a trout's, with a long body and a forked tail.

- **Length:** 19 to 48 inches (48.3 to 121.9 cm)
- **Weight:** 40 to 72 pounds (18.1 to 32.7 kg)
- **Lifespan:** 12 to 41 years
- **Conservation Status:** Least Concern

HABITAT & DIET

The lake trout lives in freshwater lakes of North America, usually deeper than 50 feet (15.2 m). Younger trout mostly eat insects, plankton, and invertebrates. Adult trout often eat bigger fish.

FAMILY & SOCIAL LIFE

Lake trout spawn among rocks in water currents. A female lays 2,000 to 20,000 eggs at a time.

DID YOU KNOW?

Lake trout are most often found in water between 40°F and 50°F (4.4°C and 10°C).

LAMPREY

ALL ABOUT

Lampreys are jawless, cartilaginous fish that have a round, suction-cup mouth lined with sharp teeth. Pacific lampreys live along the Pacific coast, whereas sea lampreys come from the Atlantic coast.

- **Length:** 13 to 33 inches (33 to 83.8 cm)
- **Weight:** up to 1 pound (0.5 kg)
- **Lifespan:** up to 13 years
- **Conservation Status:** Least Concern

DID YOU KNOW?

Sea lampreys have traveled into the Great Lakes. There, they have killed many lake fish which, unlike ocean fish, cannot survive the lamprey's parasitic behavior.

HABITAT & DIET

Lampreys spawn in freshwater streams. Their larvae, which don't have eyes or teeth, act similar to earthworms. They burrow into the ground and stay there for three to seven years. They poke their head out to eat floating algae.

FUN FACT

Lampreys have existed on Earth for more than 360 million years.

FAMILY & SOCIAL LIFE

As a lamprey grows into a juvenile, it grows eyes and teeth and then migrates to the ocean where it becomes a parasite. The lamprey attaches its mouth to a fish or a whale, sucking the animal's blood and other fluids without killing it. After one to six years, the lamprey becomes an adult and returns to fresh water. After laying up to 100,000 eggs, the female, along with her mate, dies.

LUMPSUCKER

ALL ABOUT

Lumpsuckers are shaped like bumpy ping-pong balls. One fin acts like a suction cup, allowing the fish to attach to rocks or plants.

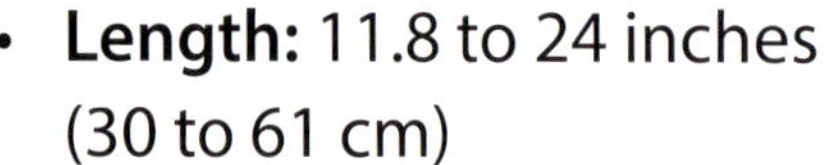

- **Length:** 11.8 to 24 inches (30 to 61 cm)
- **Weight:** up to 13 pounds (5.9 kg)
- **Lifespan:** up to 15 years
- **Conservation Status:** Data Deficient

DID YOU KNOW?

Male lumpsuckers turn reddish orange during spawning season. Females turn bluish green.

HABITAT & DIET

The lumpsucker eats shrimp, jellyfish, and small fish. Adults spend winters at sea, close to the rocky ocean floor. They can live in water up to 5,600 feet (1,706.9 m) deep.

FAMILY & SOCIAL LIFE

Lumpsuckers migrate closer to shore to breed. The female deposits eggs in kelp beds and then goes back out to sea. The male attaches itself to a nearby rock for eight weeks until the eggs hatch.

NINESPINE STICKLEBACK

ALL ABOUT

The ninespine stickleback is a small white-bellied fish with a line of spines on its back.

- **Length:** up to 3.5 inches (8.9 cm)
- **Weight:** 0.02 to 0.06 ounces (0.6 to 1.7 g)
- **Lifespan:** up to 5 years
- **Conservation Status:** Least Concern

HABITAT & DIET

Some of these fish live in freshwater lakes around the Arctic, whereas others live in the ocean, close to shore. This fish eats mostly insects and crustaceans, especially amphipods.

FAMILY & SOCIAL LIFE

In summer, the male builds a tunnel-shaped nest, using a liquid from his body to hold the nest together. The female deposits eggs and then leaves. The male fertilizes the eggs and then protects the eggs and young for about two weeks after hatching.

FUN FACT

Despite the ninespine stickleback's name, the spines on this tiny fish can number from 8 to 11.

NORTHERN PIKE

ALL ABOUT

The northern pike is a long, thin fish with numerous sharp teeth. It is an ambush hunter and will lunge quickly to attack prey.

- **Length:** up to 4.5 feet (1.4 m)
- **Weight:** 2 to 62 pounds (0.9 to 28.1 kg)
- **Lifespan:** 10 to 20 years
- **Conservation Status:** Least Concern

DID YOU KNOW?

Northern pike can crossbreed with a fish called the muskellunge. The hybrid fish is known as a tiger musky.

HABITAT & DIET

Northern pike live in freshwater lakes, streams, and ponds across the Arctic. These fierce predators eat fish, snakes, birds, frogs, and mice.

FAMILY & SOCIAL LIFE

Over 5 to 10 days, a female releases up to 250,000 eggs, which attach to plants. Warmer water temperatures make the eggs hatch faster. But if the water gets warmer than 60°F (15.6°C), the young often don't survive.

ROCK GUNNEL

ALL ABOUT

The rock gunnel is a long eel-like fish. It's usually yellowish or brown, with 9 to 15 black spots on its back.

- **Length:** 6.7 to 9.8 inches (17 to 24.9 cm)
- **Weight:** 0.09 to 0.5 ounces (2.6 to 14.2 g)
- **Lifespan:** 1.2 to 5 years
- **Conservation Status:** Least Concern

FUN FACT

The rock gunnel is sometimes called a butterfish due to its slippery skin.

HABITAT & DIET

This fish lives along rocky shorelines of the northern Atlantic Ocean. It eats crustaceans, mollusks, and marine worms. It hides in seaweed and under rocks. The rock gunnel can survive out of water during low tide, when it breathes air.

FAMILY & SOCIAL LIFE

This fish spawns in the winter. The parents take turns guarding their eggs, which are laid in groups of 80 to 200.

SALMON

ALL ABOUT

Chum and pink salmon are two kinds of salmon that live in the Arctic. The chum is one of the biggest salmon, whereas the pink is the smallest. Both types die after spawning.

- **Length:** 20 to 43.2 inches (50.8 to 109.7 cm)
- **Weight:** 3.5 to 35 pounds (1.6 to 15.9 kg)
- **Lifespan:** 2 to 6 years
- **Conservation Status:** Not Assessed

HABITAT & DIET

Pink salmon eat krill, plankton, shrimp, and small fish in the ocean. Chum salmon eat insects, invertebrates, copepods, fish, and mollusks. Salmon live in the ocean until they're ready to spawn. During this time, the fish do not eat.

DID YOU KNOW?

When male chum salmon are ready to spawn, they turn brown with red-purple stripes and grow fangs.

Chum salmon

FAMILY & SOCIAL LIFE

Most salmon return to the freshwater river where they hatched to have their own young. In the fall, the fish swim upstream to spawn. Sometimes this journey includes jumping up waterfalls. The females dig nests in gravel for their eggs. Eggs hatch several months later. Young fish may eat insects on their swim to the ocean.

Pink salmon

FUN FACT

Male pink salmon are nicknamed humpback salmon for the hump that grows on their back during spawning.

Pink salmon

SHORTHORN SCULPIN

ALL ABOUT

The shorthorn sculpin has spiny, flat scales on its back. It also has spines on its head and behind its eyes. Like other sculpin, proteins in its blood prevent this fish from freezing in its Arctic environment.

- **Length:** up to 18 inches (45.7 cm)
- **Weight:** up to 2.2 pounds (1 kg)
- **Lifespan:** 9 to 15 years
- **Conservation Status:** Not Assessed

HABITAT & DIET

The shorthorn sculpin lives in cold water near the ocean floor, among seaweed, mud, or sand. It eats mostly fish and crustaceans. It lies still to wait for prey to pass, then attacks.

FAMILY & SOCIAL LIFE

This fish lays red or yellow eggs in groups among rocks. Males guard the eggs.

FUN FACT

Shorthorn sculpins are red or copper colored. Males become much brighter during mating season.

THORNY SKATE

ALL ABOUT

The thorny skate is sometimes called a starry ray. This flat, brown, square-shaped fish has a long, thin tail and up to 20 thorns on its back.

- **Length:** 17.7 to 40.2 inches (45 to 102.1 cm)
- **Weight:** up to 25 pounds (11.3 g)
- **Lifespan:** up to 28 years
- **Conservation Status:** Vulnerable

FUN FACT

Each thorny skate egg is laid in a capsule nicknamed a mermaid's purse, which attaches to rocks or seaweed.

HABITAT & DIET

The thorny skate eats worms, crustaceans, and fish, including crabs, shrimp, cod, and eel. It lives on the bottom of the ocean, in water at least 59 feet (18 m) deep.

FAMILY & SOCIAL LIFE

The thorny skate is fully grown at about 11 years. Females produce eggs year-round.

THREESPINE STICKLEBACK

ALL ABOUT

The tiny threespine stickleback has protective bony plates on its sides. In places with many predators, these fish can grow additional plates to adapt to its more dangerous environment.

- **Length:** up to 3.9 inches (9.9 cm)
- **Weight:** 0.04 to 0.08 ounces (1.1 to 2.3 g)
- **Lifespan:** up to 4 years
- **Conservation Status:** Least Concern

HABITAT & DIET

This stickleback lives in salt water until breeding season. Then it swims to shallow freshwater streams. It eats insect larvae, small fish, worms, and crustaceans.

FAMILY & SOCIAL LIFE

The male builds a nest of plants using a sticky substance from his body. Several females may lay eggs in the nest. Then he guards the eggs and protects the young.

FUN FACT

Threespine sticklebacks use their spines and threatening body postures to scare away predators.

WALLEYE POLLOCK

ALL ABOUT

The walleye pollock is a type of cod. Younger fish tend to stay closer to the surface than older fish.

- **Length:** up to 3.4 feet (1 m)
- **Weight:** up to 13.3 pounds (6 kg)
- **Lifespan:** 15 to 20 years
- **Conservation Status:** Near Threatened

DID YOU KNOW?

Walleye pollock eggs take longer to hatch in colder water.

HABITAT & DIET

These fish eat copepods, crustaceans, plankton, their own eggs, and sometimes other walleye pollock. Outside of breeding season, the walleye pollock live in deep water, usually between 330 and 985 feet (100.6 and 300.2 m), near continental shelves.

FAMILY & SOCIAL LIFE

In late winter and early spring, these fish form large schools for spawning. They migrate to shallow water. Eggs and hatched fish float near the surface.

ADDITIONAL FISH

Arctic eelpout

ARCTIC EELPOUT

- **About:** These fish scrape the ocean floor with their lower jaw to find prey.
- **Habitat:** near cold-water ocean floors
- **Conservation Status:** Not Assessed

ARCTIC SAND LANCE

- **About:** Their long, thin bodies make it easy for them to dive into sandy ground.
- **Habitat:** shallow, sandy ocean floor
- **Conservation Status:** Data Deficient

ARCTIC SKATE

- **About:** This fish has a short tail and 22 to 31 spines along its back.
- **Habitat:** ocean floor in cold water
- **Conservation Status:** Least Concern

Arctic skate

LAKE WHITEFISH

- **About:** The oldest lake whitefish on record was 50 years old.
- **Habitat:** cold freshwater lakes
- **Conservation Status:** Not Assessed

Lake whitefish

NORTHEAST ARCTIC HADDOCK

- **About:** This fish scatters its eggs in deep water.
- **Habitat:** cold ocean water
- **Conservation Status:** Vulnerable

PACIFIC SLEEPER SHARK

- **About:** These slow-moving sharks eat many kinds of ocean animals, including seals.
- **Habitat:** deep, cold ocean water
- **Conservation Status:** Near Threatened

SNAILFISH

- **About:** These long, soft fish have loose skin with no scales.
- **Habitat:** cold ocean water
- **Conservation Status:** Data Deficient

Snailfish

AMPHIBIANS

Amphibians are cold-blooded vertebrates. Their body temperature fluctuates with their surroundings. These animals live both on land and in water. They usually have damp skin but no scales. Salamanders, frogs, and newts are all amphibians.

Most amphibians lay eggs in water. But some give birth to live young. The only amphibian that lives in the Arctic is the wood frog.

WOOD FROG

ALL ABOUT

During the winter, wood frogs burrow into dead leaves. Their bodies make a substance that prevents their cells from freezing. But in the space between the frog's cells, ice forms. As a result, the frog's heart stops beating, and the frog stops breathing. In the spring, the wood frog thaws.

- **Length:** 1.5 to 3.3 inches (3.8 to 8.4 cm)
- **Weight:** up to 0.3 ounces (8.5 g)
- **Lifespan:** up to 3 years
- **Conservation Status:** Least Concern

FUN FACT

In large groups, wood frog tadpoles can identify their siblings and gather together.

HABITAT & DIET

Tadpoles mostly eat algae, but they sometimes eat amphibian larvae. Adults eat snails, slugs, insects, arachnids, and worms.

FAMILY & SOCIAL LIFE

The female lays 1,000 to 3,000 eggs at a time. They hatch within 30 days.

INSECTS AND ARACHNIDS

Jutta Arctic/ Baltic grayling

Scientists believe that there may be five million different insect species on Earth, living in every type of habitat. There are more insects than any other type of animal. Insects are a type of invertebrate called arthropods. They have exoskeletons, which are skeletons or shells on the outside of their body.

The body of an insect has three main parts: a head, an abdomen, and a thorax. Most insects have six legs that are attached to the thorax. An insect's abdomen holds its bodily systems and organs. Most insects begin life as larvae before turning into adults.

Arachnids are also arthropods with exoskeletons. But arachnids keep the same basic body shape their entire life. Most arachnids have eight legs and live on land, whereas insects can be found both on land and in water.

Arctic fritillary

ARCTIC BUMBLEBEE

ALL ABOUT

The Arctic bumblebee has thick hair to keep it warm. Additionally, it can increase its body temperature by vibrating its flying muscles.

- **Length:** 0.4 inches (1 cm)
- **Weight:** 0.001 to 1.1 ounces (0.03 to 31.2 g)
- **Lifespan:** 3 to 12 months
- **Conservation Status:** Data Deficient

HABITAT & DIET

The queen bumblebee builds an insulated nest from wax and pollen. All bees in the hive eat nectar.

FAMILY & SOCIAL LIFE

Each hive has one queen per year, along with worker bees. The queen lays several clutches of eggs during her short life. One queen in each colony can survive the winter. The other bees die when winter comes.

DID YOU KNOW?

Arctic bumblebees warm their bodies by resting on cone-shaped flowers, which reflect warm sunlight into their centers.

ARCTIC FRITILLARY

ALL ABOUT

The Arctic fritillary has orange wings with black markings. Fritillaries are small butterflies. They don't have claws on their front legs, as most butterflies do.

- **Wingspan:** 1.2 to 1.5 inches (3 to 3.8 cm)
- **Weight:** not enough data
- **Lifespan:** up to 2 years
- **Conservation Status:** Near Threatened

HABITAT & DIET

This butterfly lives in tundra, forests, bogs, and mountain meadows. Adult Arctic fritillaries eat nectar from goldenrod and aster flowers. Caterpillars eat scrub willow plants and violets.

FAMILY & SOCIAL LIFE

Females lay their eggs on the bottom side of leaves. Caterpillars hatch in 6 to 10 days. They eat the leaves of the plant where their eggs were laid.

FUN FACT

In the Arctic, this insect hibernates as a caterpillar for two winters before changing into a butterfly.

ARCTIC MOSQUITO

ALL ABOUT

Arctic mosquitoes are the most important pollinators in the Arctic.

- **Length:** 0.1 to 0.8 inches (0.3 to 2 cm)
- **Weight:** 1/15,000 ounce (2 mg)
- **Lifespan:** up to 9 weeks
- **Conservation Status:** Not Assessed

HABITAT & DIET

Larvae eat microbes on waste and dead plants in ponds. Adult males eat pollen and nectar. Adult females feed on nectar and animal blood, mostly of caribou.

FAMILY & SOCIAL LIFE

Arctic mosquitoes lay eggs in ponds that freeze in winter. When the ponds melt in spring, the eggs hatch. They are larvae for two to three weeks before changing into adult mosquitoes.

FUN FACT

In summer, the Arctic has a greater concentration of mosquitoes than anywhere else in the world.

BRISTLETAIL

ALL ABOUT

The bristletail's tail has three long, narrow parts. Each piece is bristled, or covered in short, coarse hair. The bristletail is wingless and can't fly, but it can jump as high as 6 inches (15.2 cm).

- **Length:** up to 0.8 inches (2 cm)
- **Weight:** not enough data
- **Lifespan:** up to 4 years
- **Conservation Status:** Not Assessed

DID YOU KNOW?

The bristletail molts several times in its life by attaching itself with poop to something hard before sliding out of its exoskeleton.

HABITAT & DIET

Bristletails are most active at night. They live in rocky crevices near ocean shorelines. They eat soft plants, such as moss, lichens, and algae.

FAMILY & SOCIAL LIFE

At the end of summer, the bristletail lays eggs in mossy rock areas. The eggs do not hatch until the following spring.

ISABELLA TIGER MOTH

ALL ABOUT

The Isabella tiger moth is called a woolly bear or woolly worm when it is in its larval stage. The caterpillar has black ends and a brownish-red middle. It has stiff, fuzzy hairs on its body. As it gets older, it becomes more red and less black.

- **Wingspan:** 1.8 to 2.3 inches (4.6 to 5.8 cm)
- **Weight:** not enough data
- **Lifespan:** under 1 year
- **Conservation Status:** Not Assessed

FUN FACT

The Isabella tiger moth caterpillar can survive extremely cold temperatures, down to –90°F (–67.8°C).

HABITAT & DIET

The caterpillar eats plants including birch, asters, sunflowers, clovers, and maple. Adult moths eat nectar from flowers. The moths are more active at night. These insects live in the Arctic, but they also live in many parts of North America.

DID YOU KNOW?

Very wet weather can cause the Isabella tiger moth caterpillar to have coloring that is more black than red.

FAMILY & SOCIAL LIFE

An Isabella tiger moth lays two groups of eggs. The first group of larvae builds cocoons to transform into moths in summer. The second group of larvae remains caterpillars through the winter. They hide under piles of leaves or wood. In the spring, they wake from hibernation. Then those larvae transform into moths.

MILLER MOTH

ALL ABOUT

As a caterpillar, the miller moth is green. It is covered with long whitish-green hairs. Several different species of moths around the world are called miller moths. The adult stage of all miller moths looks similar, but their larvae look different. This moth's scientific name is *Acronicta leporina*. The first word means "nightfall." The second means "hare in winter."

- **Wingspan:** 1.4 to 1.8 inches (3.6 to 4.6 cm)
- **Weight:** not enough data
- **Lifespan:** 1 year
- **Conservation Status:** Not Assessed

HABITAT & DIET

This species lives mostly in northern Europe. It's most common in wooded areas and shrubland. The larvae eat parts of trees, including birch, poplar, beech, and oak.

FAMILY & SOCIAL LIFE

The caterpillar forms a cocoon under the bark of a tree. It builds the cocoon in late fall and stays in it until spring. Adult moths live from about June through August. They are more active at night.

DID YOU KNOW?

Many moths and butterflies die within a few weeks. The miller moth can live for up to four months.

NORTHERN CLOUDED YELLOW

ALL ABOUT

The northern clouded yellow is a type of sulphur butterfly. All sulphurs have yellow wings. Also called the Arctic sulphur, the northern clouded yellow has pale yellow wings with reddish edges. Females are larger than males.

- **Wingspan:** 1.4 to 1.8 inches (3.6 to 4.6 cm)
- **Weight:** not enough data
- **Lifespan:** a few weeks to a few months
- **Conservation Status:** Near Threatened

FUN FACT

When this butterfly is resting, it presses its wings together.

HABITAT & DIET

This butterfly lives in damp tundra areas and along riverbanks that have many plants. Larvae of the northern clouded yellow eat the astragalus plant and the Arctic willow.

FAMILY & SOCIAL LIFE

Butterflies live from June to August. Females lay eggs one at a time on plant leaves.

POLARIS FRITILLARY

ALL ABOUT

The Polaris fritillary is a kind of brush-footed butterfly, which has small and hairy front legs. These butterflies use their other four legs to walk.

- **Wingspan:** 1.4 to 1.8 inches (3.6 to 4.6 cm)
- **Weight:** not enough data
- **Lifespan:** up to 2 years
- **Conservation Status:** Vulnerable

HABITAT & DIET

The larvae of the Polaris fritillary eat leaves and flowers. Adult butterflies eat nectar. This butterfly lives north of the tree line.

FUN FACT

"Fritillary" comes from the Latin word *fritillus*, which means "chessboard."

FAMILY & SOCIAL LIFE

The caterpillar hatches in late fall. It lives through the winter and then changes into a butterfly in the spring. The butterfly lives from late June into early July.

REINDEER WARBLE FLY

ALL ABOUT

The larvae of the reindeer warble fly are parasites and feed off of reindeer, which are also called caribou. The larvae are usually yellowish white.

- **Length (larvae):** up to 1 inch (2.5 cm)
- **Weight:** not enough data
- **Lifespan:** less than 1 year
- **Conservation Status:** Not Assessed

HABITAT & DIET

The reindeer warble fly lives with caribou throughout the Arctic tundra. Adult reindeer warble flies do not eat.

FAMILY & SOCIAL LIFE

Females lay their eggs in caribou fur. When the larvae hatch, they burrow into the caribou's skin where they feed and grow for several months. When big enough, the larvae chew a hole through the skin to come out.

FUN FACT

Reindeer warble fly larvae are also called maggots.

WOODLAND RINGLET

ALL ABOUT

The woodland ringlet is a butterfly with small rings on its brown wings. These markings are sometimes described as eye spots.

- **Wingspan:** 1.3 to 1.7 inches (3.3 to 4.3 cm)
- **Weight:** not enough data
- **Lifespan:** 1 year
- **Conservation Status:** Least Concern

HABITAT & DIET

The woodland ringlet lives in woodlands and meadows. Larvae eat plants, especially thick grass. The adult butterfly eats nectar from buttercups, cow parsley, clovers, and thistles.

FAMILY & SOCIAL LIFE

Females lay eggs in fall. The insects hatch and remain as caterpillars through the winter. In late spring or early summer, they transform into butterflies.

FUN FACT

The underside of the woodland ringlet's wings looks the same as the topside.

ADDITIONAL INSECTS AND ARACHNIDS

AMARA ALPINA

- **About:** This ground beetle eats dead insects.
- **Habitat:** cold, dry meadows with high elevation
- **Conservation Status:** Not Assessed

ARCTIC WOLF SPIDER

- **About:** Arctic wolf spiders sometimes eat one another, including their babies.
- **Habitat:** tundra
- **Conservation Status:** Not Assessed

CADDISFLY

- **About:** Larvae produce silky threads to protect themselves and catch food.
- **Habitat:** near freshwater sources
- **Conservation Status:** Some species are threatened.

COLIAS TYCHE

- **About:** This butterfly's name comes from the god of luck in Greek mythology.
- **Habitat:** mountain tundra
- **Conservation Status:** Least Concern

DUSKY WINGED FRITILLARY

- **About:** This insect spends two winters as a caterpillar before turning into a butterfly.
- **Habitat:** tundra
- **Conservation Status:** Endangered

Colias tyche

Caddisfly

Dusky winged fritillary

JUTTA ARCTIC/BALTIC GRAYLING

- **About:** This butterfly drops its eggs loosely around a host plant.
- **Habitat:** wet tundra, spruce bogs, pine forest
- **Conservation Status:** Least Concern

MIDGE

- **About:** The midge's bright red larvae are often called bloodworms.
- **Habitat:** near ponds and streams
- **Conservation Status:** Least Concern to Critically Endangered

PARASITOID WASP

- **About:** These insects lay their eggs inside other insects.
- **Habitat:** around flowers, leaves, and plants
- **Conservation Status:** Not Assessed

Jutta Arctic/ Baltic grayling

MARINE INVERTEBRATES

Invertebrates are cold-blooded animals without vertebrae, or backbones. They also don't have bony skeletons. There are far more invertebrates than vertebrates on Earth. In fact, invertebrates make up more than 90 percent of all animals.

Most invertebrates don't have much in common with one another. They vary widely in appearance. They can have soft bodies or hard exoskeletons. Sizes can range from more than 1,000 pounds (453.6 kg) to smaller than what can be seen with the human eye. Jellyfish, lobsters, snails, clams, worms, squid, octopuses, and sea urchins are all invertebrates.

The European lobster is also known as the common lobster.

The highly toxic lion's mane jellyfish is the largest jellyfish in the world.

Invertebrates live in a variety of habitats and climates, from hot to cold and from dry to wet. Most Arctic invertebrates live in cold oceans. Many of them are low on the food chain and serve as an important food source for other animals.

ACORN BARNACLE

ALL ABOUT

An acorn barnacle starts life as a swimming larva. It then attaches to a hard surface, such as a rock. Its body makes a cement to help it stick. The barnacle grows a protective shell.

- **Length:** 0.8 to 4 inches (2 to 10.2 cm)
- **Weight:** not enough data
- **Lifespan:** 8 to 10 years
- **Conservation Status:** Not Assessed

HABITAT & DIET

The acorn barnacle lives on rocky ocean coastlines throughout the northern Atlantic and Pacific Oceans. It filter feeds on plankton and floating waste.

FAMILY & SOCIAL LIFE

Acorn barnacles have both male and female organs. They can both make their own eggs and fertilize others' eggs, which grow within the barnacle's shell.

DID YOU KNOW?

The acorn barnacle closes its shell to avoid drying out when the water level is low.

AMPHIPOD

FUN FACT

Amphipods often swim on their sides.

ALL ABOUT

An amphipod is a small shrimp-like crustacean. It has claws that can grip and antennae that are as long as its body.

- **Length:** up to 1.6 inches (4.1 cm)
- **Weight:** 0.003 to 0.01 ounces (0.09 to 0.3 g)
- **Lifespan:** 3 to 5 years
- **Conservation Status:** Not Assessed

HABITAT & DIET

The amphipod eats algae and invertebrates, which it captures with its front legs. The amphipods in the Arctic live under sea ice or on the ocean floor.

FAMILY & SOCIAL LIFE

The female lays a few hundred eggs into a pouch, where they hatch one to three weeks later. The hatchlings leave the pouch within a few days.

COPEPOD

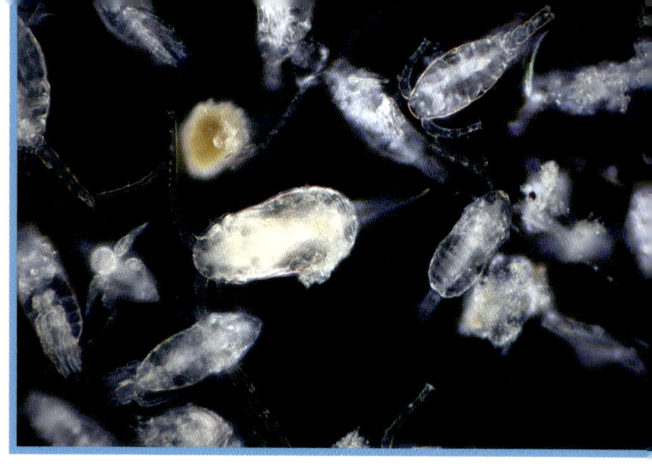

ALL ABOUT

Copepods are tiny crustaceans. They are nicknamed insects of the sea. The word *copepod* means "oar-footed." They use their feet and legs as oars.

- **Length:** 0.1 to 0.8 inches (0.3 to 2 cm)
- **Weight:** not enough data
- **Lifespan:** 6 months to 3 years
- **Conservation Status:** Not Assessed

FUN FACT

Arctic copepods build up fat to help them survive cold temperatures.

HABITAT & DIET

In the Arctic, copepods live under sea ice, on the ocean floor, or in the water in between. They are filter feeders and eat bacteria and algae.

FAMILY & SOCIAL LIFE

Females lay eggs loose in the water or into a little pouch on their bodies. As copepods grow, they shed their shells and grow new ones. This happens many times over their lifetime.

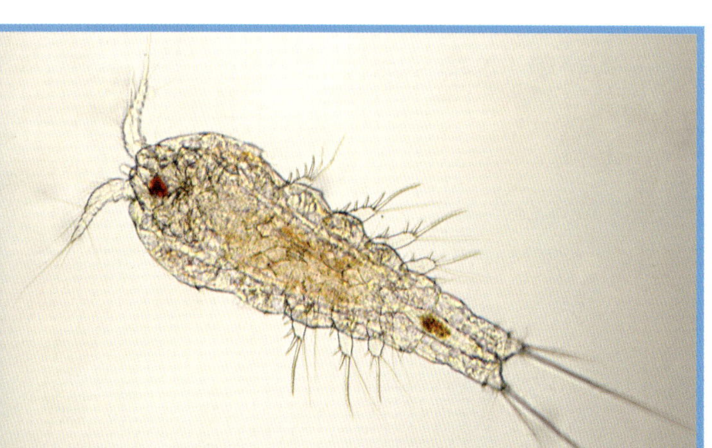

KRILL

ALL ABOUT

Krill are tiny shrimp-like crustaceans. Their legs look like feathers, but they work like fish fins.

- **Length:** up to 2.5 inches (6.4 cm)
- **Weight:** less than 0.04 ounces (1.1 g)
- **Lifespan:** about 2 years
- **Conservation Status:** Not Assessed

DID YOU KNOW?

If a big group of krill is disturbed, they scatter. Some of the krill leave their exoskeletons behind.

HABITAT & DIET

During the day, krill stay in deep water to protect themselves from predators. At night, krill float to the surface to eat plankton and tiny plants.

FAMILY & SOCIAL LIFE

Most krill lay eggs into the water where they float until they hatch. Krill molt as they grow, shedding their old exoskeletons and making new, larger ones. Krill are usually found in large schools that can have tens of thousands of individuals.

LION'S MANE JELLY

ALL ABOUT

The lion's mane jelly is the largest on Earth. Its bell can be up to 8 feet (2.4 m) across. This jelly is usually orange, red, or yellow. It has a deadly poison in its tentacles, which sting anything they touch.

- **Length (with tentacles):** more than 100 feet (30.5 m)
- **Weight:** 200 to 480 pounds (90.7 to 217.7 kg)
- **Lifespan:** 1 year
- **Conservation Status:** Not Assessed

FUN FACT

The lion's mane jelly is bioluminescent, meaning it can make its own light.

HABITAT & DIET

This creature lives in cold ocean water. Bigger jellies tend to live farther north. The lion's mane jelly eats zooplankton, small fish and crustaceans, and moon jellies. The sting of the jelly's tentacles paralyzes its prey. The tentacles then guide the prey to the jelly's mouth.

FAMILY & SOCIAL LIFE

Several kinds of fish help clean arthropods from this jelly. In exchange, the fish shelter under the jelly or among its tentacles for protection.

Jelly larvae attach to the ocean floor. When conditions are right, they let go and grow into adults.

DID YOU KNOW?

Leatherbacks and other sea turtles prey upon the lion's mane jelly. The turtles do not seem affected by the jelly's sting.

SKELETON SHRIMP

ALL ABOUT

Skeleton shrimp are a type of crustacean. They have three pairs of legs on the back part of their bodies and two pairs at the front. They use their front legs for defense and to collect food. Their rear legs help them attach to algae and sponges. Male skeleton shrimp are much larger than females.

- **Length:** up to 1.5 inches (3.8 cm)
- **Weight:** not enough data
- **Lifespan:** 1 year
- **Conservation Status:** Not Assessed

DID YOU KNOW?

Skeleton shrimp are sometimes called the praying mantises of the sea, due to their similar appearance to the land creatures.

HABITAT & DIET

These small creatures use their two pairs of antennae to filter food, which includes other amphipods, waste, and microscopic plants. The antennae also help them swim. Skeleton shrimp can be found in a range of habitats, including the deep sea of the Arctic.

FUN FACT

Some skeleton shrimp can change color, helping them hide from predators.

FAMILY & SOCIAL LIFE

Skeleton shrimp molt their exoskeletons as they grow. They mate when a female is between exoskeletons. Some female skeleton shrimp, but not all, kill the male after mating. The female keeps the eggs in a pouch on her body. When the young hatch, they are fully formed.

SNOW CRAB

ALL ABOUT

The snow crab has eight legs and two claws. It has a hard exoskeleton, which it molts as the crab grows. Until the new shell hardens, the crab is not protected from predators.

- **Length:** 3 to 6 inches (7.6 to 15.2 cm)
- **Weight:** about 1.9 pounds (0.9 kg)
- **Lifespan:** up to 20 years
- **Conservation Status:** Not Assessed

HABITAT & DIET

In the Arctic, snow crabs can be found around Alaska, northern Russia, Greenland, and northern Canada. They live mostly in cold water, usually less than 650 feet (198.1 m) deep. They tend to stay on the ocean floor where they burrow into the sand or mud to hide from predators and to find food. Their larvae eat plankton. Older crabs eat fish, shrimp, worms, snails, algae, and sponges, as well as dead creatures.

FAMILY & SOCIAL LIFE

When the crab is fully grown, it sheds and reforms its final shell. A female's last shell has a place to hold up to 100,000 eggs. The eggs hatch in springtime, when there's plenty of food for the larvae.

DID YOU KNOW?

The snow crab population has dropped dramatically in recent years as a result of warming ocean waters. In Alaska, fishing for snow crabs has been banned to allow their population to recover.

FUN FACT

Most snow crabs will have 10 to 14 molts throughout their lifetime.

ADDITIONAL MARINE INVERTEBRATES

ARCTIC MOON SNAIL

- **About:** This snail covers its prey and then pokes a hole in its shell to extract it.
- **Habitat:** shallow ocean shores
- **Conservation Status:** Not Assessed

European lobster

CUMACEAN

- **About:** Cumaceans carry their eggs and young in a pouch on their bodies.
- **Habitat:** muddy or sandy ocean floors
- **Conservation Status:** Not Assessed

Cumacean

EUROPEAN LOBSTER

- **About:** This clawed lobster is bluish green or greenish black.
- **Habitat:** ocean floor
- **Conservation Status:** Least Concern

ICE WORMS

- **About:** Ice worms can only live in temperatures close to freezing.
- **Habitat:** inside glaciers and on snowfields
- **Conservation Status:** Not Assessed

Mya truncata

SEA SQUIRT

- **About:** This creature produces a thick substance that surrounds and protects it.
- **Habitat:** ocean floor
- **Conservation Status:** Not Assessed

MYA TRUNCATA

- **About:** The mya truncata is a bivalve, or clam, that burrows into mud.
- **Habitat:** ocean floor
- **Conservation Status:** Not Assessed

Sea squirt

Toad crab

TOAD CRAB

- **About:** A type of spider crab, toad crabs often live in the same areas as snow crabs.
- **Habitat:** ocean floor
- **Conservation Status:** Least Concern

GLOSSARY

alpha
The leader of a group of animals.

arthropod
A type of animal with a segmented body, jointed limbs, and an exoskeleton.

calf
The name for the young of certain animals, including seals and whales.

carrion
Dead and decaying flesh.

cephalopod
An ocean animal with tentacles coming from its head.

crop
A pouch in a bird's throat that stores food.

crustacean
An ocean animal that has an exoskeleton.

down
The soft feathers closest to a bird's skin.

esophagus
The tube that moves food from an animal's mouth to its stomach.

Eurasia
The combined landmass of Europe and Asia.

fluctuate
To change often.

incubation
The period of keeping eggs warm until they hatch.

larvae
Insects at an early stage of life, between the stages of egg and pupa.

migrate
To move from one area or climate to another during a certain time of year.

molt
To drop or lose feathers or an exoskeleton before growing new ones.

parasite
A plant or animal that lives inside or on the body of another animal or plant.

pod
A group of some kinds of ocean animals, including dolphins, whales, and seals.

scat
Animal droppings or feces.

spawn
To produce many eggs or young.

upwelling
The process of cold, deep ocean water pushing up toward the surface.

zooplankton
Tiny creatures that float in the ocean.

TO LEARN MORE

FURTHER READINGS

DK. *Eyewitness Arctic and Antarctic*. DK, 2024.

Golkar, Golriz. *Freshwater Fish*. Abdo Reference, 2024.

London, Martha. *The Effects of Climate Change*. Abdo Publishing, 2021.

Rusick, Jessica. *Surviving the Arctic*. Abdo Publishing, 2024.

Wheeler, Jill C. *Extreme Cold: Survival Stories*. Abdo Publishing, 2024.

ONLINE RESOURCES

To learn more about Arctic animals, please visit **abdobooklinks.com** or scan this QR code. These links are routinely monitored and updated to provide the most current information available.

INDEX

PHOTO CREDITS

Cover Photos: Martin Hejzlar/Shutterstock, front (musk ox); FedBul/iStock/Getty Images, front (char); Sylvie Bouchard/Shutterstock, front (caribou); HHelene/Shutterstock, front (miller moth); clarst5/Shutterstock, front (snowy owl); FloridaStock/Shutterstock, front (polar bear); Eric Isselee/Shutterstock, front (harbor seal), front (Atlantic puffin), front (Eurasian otter), back (Arctic fox); Chase D'Animulls/Adobe Stock, front (Canada lynx); ericlefrancais/Shutterstock, back (walrus); Rob Palmer Photography/Shutterstock, back (gyrfalcon)

Interior Photos: FotoRequest/Shutterstock, 1, 125; Michal Ninger/Shutterstock, 3, 34 (bottom); Robert Harding Video/Shutterstock, 4; Incredible Arctic/Shutterstock, 5; Andrei Stepanov/Shutterstock, 6, 58, 59 (bottom); Designua/Shutterstock, 7; Alexey Seafarer/Shutterstock, 8; Maridav/Shutterstock, 9; Sergey Uryadnikov/Shutterstock, 10; Vicki Beaver, Alaska Fisheries Science Center, NOAA FIsheries, Marine Mammal Permit #14245/Wikimedia Commons, 11; Susan E. Adams/Wikimedia Commons, 12 (top); Gerald Corsi/iStock/Getty Images, 12 (bottom), 71 (bottom), 179 (top); Colin Seddon/Shutterstock, 13 (top); Vaclav Matous/Shutterstock, 13 (bottom); AndreAnita/Shutterstock, 14, 102 (top), 109; Dolores M. Harvey/Shutterstock, 15; Fred Bruemmer/Stockbyte/Getty Images, 16; Enrique Aguirre Aves/Photodisc/Getty Images, 17; John K. B. Ford/Ursus/Blue Planet Archive, 18; Doc White/Blue Planet Archive, 19; MuhammadIshfaq1/Shutterstock, 20; MuhammadHanif1/Shutterstock, 21; Jane Rix/Shutterstock, 22; evaurban/Shutterstock, 23; Josh London/Bering Land Bridge National Preserve/Flickr, 24; Marcelorpc/Shutterstock, 25 (top); Gerald Corsi/E+/Getty Images, 25 (bottom); Valerijs Novickis/Shutterstock, 26; Moelyn Photos/Moment/Getty Images, 27; torstenvelden/RooM/Getty Images, 28–29; lisnic/Shutterstock, 30; Andrea Izzotti/Shutterstock, 31; Robert Postma/Design Pics/Getty Images, 32; Ondrej Prosicky/Shutterstock, 33, 129; Ludek Krona Kroneisl/Shutterstock, 34 (top); Darrell Gulin/The Image Bank/Getty Images, 35 (top); mlorenzphotography/Moment/Getty Images, 35 (bottom); KenCanning/iStock/Getty Images, 36; Tomas Hulik ARTpoint/Shutterstock, 37, 87; Menno Schaefer/Shutterstock, 38; Mats Lindberg/Shutterstock, 39; davidhoffmann photography/Shutterstock, 40; Martin Rudlof Photography/Shutterstock, 41; Wirestock Creators/Shutterstock, 42, 46, 47, 94, 101, 169 (top); Patrick J. Endres/Corbis Documentary/Getty Images, 43; Martin Hejzlar/Shutterstock, 45, 103 (top); robertweeden/iNaturalist, 48; Bob Wick, Bureau of Land Management/Flickr, 49 (top); ALAN SCHMIERER/Flickr, 49 (bottom); Alexey Kartsev/Shutterstock, 50; Nick Pecker/Shutterstock, 51, 76 (top), 96, 102 (bottom), 111, 113, 116; Piotr Lukasik/iNaturalist, 52; Jelger Herder/Buiten-beeld/Minden Pictures, 53 (top); spatuletail/Shutterstock, 53 (bottom); Dee Carpenter Photography/iStock/Getty Images, 54 (top); Dee Carpenter Originals/Shutterstock, 54 (bottom); Henri_Lehtola/Shutterstock, 55 (top), 122 (top); Jennifer Miner/Shutterstock, 55 (bottom); Sophia Granchinho/Shutterstock, 56 (top), 56 (bottom); Piotr Krzeslak/Shutterstock, 57, 106; Jamesahanlon/Dreamstime.com, 59 (top); Scott E Read/Shutterstock, 60; Stephan Morris/Shutterstock, 61 (top); Cliff Watkinson/Shutterstock, 61 (bottom); er-birds/iNaturalist, 62 (top); MyLoupe/Universal Images Group/Getty Images, 62 (bottom); Erni/Shutterstock, 63; mikabu/Shutterstock, 64; Somogyi Laszlo/Shutterstock, 65 (top); Michal Pesata/Shutterstock, 65 (bottom), 91; Jim Cumming/Shutterstock, 66–67, 124; Nazzu/Shutterstock, 68; Dennis Jacobsen/Shutterstock, 69, 79 (bottom), 104, 105; Dubsma93/Shutterstock, 70 (top); Rosa Jay/Shutterstock, 70 (middle); McDonald Wildlife Photography Inc./Corbis/Getty Images, 70 (bottom); Maria 81/Shutterstock, 71 (top); Agami Photo Agency/Shutterstock, 72, 74 (top), 92 (top), 97, 98, 126–127; Rudmer Zwerver/Shutterstock, 73; Jukka Jantunen/Shutterstock, 74 (bottom), 77 (top), 158, 159, 161, 173 (bottom); Vishnevskiy Vasily/Shutterstock, 75; Petr Salinger/Shutterstock, 76 (bottom); Antero Aaltonen/Shutterstock, 77 (bottom); imageBROKER.com/Shutterstock, 78 (top), 114, 120; Frank Fichtmueller/Shutterstock, 78 (bottom); Mehiso/Shutterstock, 79 (top); AlekseyKarpenko/Shutterstock, 80; Gema Alvarez Fernandez/Shutterstock, 81; Greens and Blues/Shutterstock, 82; Eric Dale/Shutterstock, 82–83; Giedriius/Shutterstock, 84 (top); chris276644/Shutterstock, 84 (bottom); Lukas Zdrazil/Shutterstock, 85 (top); Andrzej Jablonski/Shutterstock, 85 (bottom); Peter Kniez/Shutterstock, 86; Michael Schroeder/Shutterstock, 88; Nicola_K_photos/Shutterstock, 89; Rob Palmer Photography/Shutterstock, 90; Pablo Rodriguez Merkel/Shutterstock, 92 (bottom); Rini Kools/Shutterstock, 93 (top), 103 (bottom); LABETAA Andre/Shutterstock, 93 (bottom); Bildagentur Zoonar GmbH/Shutterstock, 95, 172 (right); Fufachew Ivan Andreevich/Shutterstock, 99; Stephen Waycott/iStock/Getty Images, 100; Marcin Perkowski/Shutterstock, 107, 117; Roy McPeak/500px/Getty Images, 108; Leonard55/Shutterstock, 110; Wolfgang Kruck/Shutterstock, 112; rock ptarmigan/Shutterstock, 115; Maciej Olszewski/Shutterstock, 118; Keith Harvey/Shutterstock, 119; Tathoms/Shutterstock, 121; xpixel/Shutterstock, 122 (bottom), 130 (middle), (top); Gerald A. DeBoer/Shutterstock, 123 (top); Paul Reeves Photography/Shutterstock, 123 (bottom); Martin Pelanek/Shutterstock, 127; Sergey Kudryavtsev/Shutterstock, 128 (top); Cliff Day/Shutterstock, 128 (bottom); brian stahls/iNaturalist, 130 (top); Brian E Kushner/Shutterstock, 130 (bottom); Deepak Sahu/500px/500Px Plus/Getty Images, 131 (middle); Martin Mecnarowski/Shutterstock, 131 (bottom); DanBachKristensen/iStock/Getty Images, 132, 134, 135 (top); Podolnaya Elena/Shutterstock, 133; BrendanHunter/iStock/Getty Images, 135 (bottom); mlharing/iStock/Getty Images, 136; RLS Photo/Shutterstock, 137 (top), 137 (bottom), 150, 184 (bottom); LaSalle-Photo/iStock/Getty Images, 138, 155 (bottom), 180, 185; Alex Coan/Shutterstock, 139 (top), 139 (bottom); dottedhippo/iStock/Getty Images, 140; mountainpix/Shutterstock, 141 (top); Marcia Straub/Moment/Getty Images, 141 (bottom); T. Lawrence, Great Lakes Fishery Commission/NOAA Great Lakes Environmental Research Laboratory/Flickr, 142; Manuel E. Garci/Shutterstock, 143; alexkoral/Shutterstock, 144; Aleron Val/Shutterstock, 145; Kletr/Shutterstock, 146; Jeremy Brown/Dreamstime.com, 147 (top); Randy Bjorklund/Shutterstock, 147 (bottom); Nick Kashenko/Shutterstock, 148; Mike Korostelev/Moment/Getty Images, 149 (top); Paul Souders/Stone/Getty Images, 149 (bottom); Wolfgang Pölzer/Alamy, 151 (top); Steve Trewhella/imageBROKER/Newscom, 151 (bottom); slowmotiongli/iStock/Getty Images, 152; Σ64/Wikimedia Commons, 153 (top); George Berninger Jr./Wikimedia Commons, 153 (bottom); F. Hecker/picture alliance/blickwinkel/F/Newscom, 154 (top); The Hidden Ocean 2016: Chukchi Borderlands, NOAA, UAF, Oceaneering-DSSI/NOAA Ocean Exploration/Flickr, 154 (bottom); John Pennell/Dreamstime.com, 155 (top); AGabriel_Photo/Shutterstock, 156; Jason Patrick Ross/Shutterstock, 157 (top); Francis Bossé/Shutterstock, 157 (bottom); Jaume RoselloC/Shutterstock, 160; Henrik Larsson/Shutterstock, 162 (top); ErikKarits/iStock/Getty Images, 162 (bottom); Katja Schulz/Flickr, 163; Charles Brutlag/Shutterstock, 164 (top); Jay Ondreicka/Shutterstock, 164 (bottom); Jenn Forman Orth/Flickr, 165; M. Virtala/Wikimedia Commons, 166 (top); Lilly M/Wikimedia Commons, 166 (bottom); Ben Sale/Flickr, 167; Kristof Zyskowski & Yulia Bereshpolova/Cataloging Nature/Flickr, 168 (top), 168 (bottom); Matt Muir/iNaturalist, 169 (bottom); Jason Headley/iNaturalist, 170; Luca love photo/Shutterstock, 171 (top), 171 (bottom); Rasmus Holmboe Dahl/Shutterstock, 172 (left); Nils Ryrholm/C. van Swaay et al. (2012). "Dos and Don'ts for butterflies of the Habitats Directive of the European Union". Nature Conservation 1: 114. DOI:10.3897/natureconservation.1.2786/Wikimedia Commons, 173 (top); Gerald Robert Fischer/Shutterstock, 174; Stuart Westmorland/Corbis Documentary/Getty Images, 175; zmeel/iStock/Getty Images, 176; leoaleks/iStock/Getty Images, 177; CHOKSAWATDIKORN/SCIENCE PHOTO LIBRARY/Getty Images, 178 (top); NNehring/E+/Getty Images, 178 (bottom); Allexxandar/Shutterstock, 179 (bottom), 184 (top); Alexander Semenov/Moment/Getty Images, 181; Andrey Nekrasov/imageBROKER/Getty Images, 182; Alexander Semenov/Flickr, 183; Kuznetsov Petr/Shutterstock, 186 (top); Oksana_Schmidt/Shutterstock, 186 (bottom); Pataporn Kuanui/Shutterstock, 187; Andrew J. Martinez/Science Source, 187; Arterra/Universal Images Group/Getty Images, 187

ABDOBOOKS.COM
Published by Abdo Reference, a division of ABDO, PO Box 398166, Minneapolis, Minnesota 55439.

Printed in China
052025
082025

Editor: Jane Katirgis
Series Designer: Colleen McLaren

LIBRARY OF CONGRESS CONTROL NUMBER: 2024948995

PUBLISHER'S CATALOGING-IN-PUBLICATION DATA
Names: Kuehl, Ashley, author.
Title: The Arctic animal encyclopedia / by Ashley Kuehl
Description: Minneapolis, Minnesota : Abdo Reference, 2026 | Series: Animal encyclopedias | Includes online resources and index.
Identifiers: ISBN 9781098296582 (lib. bdg.) | ISBN 9798384918011 (ebook)
Subjects: LCSH: Zoology--Arctic regions--Juvenile literature. | Animals--Juvenile literature. | Animals--Behavior--Juvenile literature. | Animal habitats--Juvenile literature. | Reference materials--Juvenile literature. | Encyclopedias and dictionaries--Juvenile literature.
Classification: DDC 590.3--dc23